The Instructional Design Library

Volume 14

PROGRAMMED INSTRUCTION

Donald H. Bullock
Performance Design Corporation
McLean, Virginia

Danny G. Langdon
Series Editor

Educational Technology Publications
Englewood Cliffs, New Jersey 07632

Library of Congress Cataloging in Publication Data

Bullock, Donald H
    Programmed instruction.

    (The Instructional design library; v. no. 14)
    1. Programmed instruction. I. Title.
II. Series.
LB1028.5.B84   371.39'442   77-25108
ISBN 0-87778-118-4

Printed in the United States of America.

Library of Congress Catalog Card Number:
77-25108.

International Standard Book Number:
0-87778-118-4.

First Printing: February, 1978.
Second Printing: January, 1980.

FOREWORD

The author, Donald H. Bullock, and I are running a minor risk in including Programmed Instruction as an instructional design in this series of books. This risk comes mainly from many of our colleagues and others who would view Programmed Instruction as being more than an instructional design and, indeed, the very process by which instructional designs in general are developed and proved effective. We too recognize that Programmed Instruction does involve instructional designing, but it has a classical form or *product* labeled Programmed Instruction with which it is identified as well. Most often this product has taken the form of texts, but it may also be found in other media forms.

What I had in mind, and what the author has captured so well, in originally deciding to include PI as an instructional design, was a description of the frame-by-frame programming of a couple of decades ago. This style of programming had and has such distinctive features and merits for continued use and application, that it just had to be included, or the series would have avoided a valuable approach to learning. While we have come to our senses in recent years and now realize that PI is not a panacea—no more than any other instructional design—we have also come to realize that its classical (and modern) form has certain valid uses. The author defines these uses rather well.

In summary, Programmed Instruction is a product and it is a process. Here you will find an excellent description of the product. I dare say that no other instructional design in the Instructional Design Library has a clearer set of governing principles and practices for guiding student learning. If properly applied and validated to the right sort of needs, it can be highly effective and efficient. Applied otherwise, it is no better nor worse than any other instructional design.

Danny G. Langdon
Series Editor

PREFACE

ACKNOWLEDGMENTS

So many persons have contributed to the development of whatever competence I have *vis-a-vis* programmed instruction that it is feasible to list but a few whose support at various times during my "evolution" has been the most critical: A. Harvey Block, Stephen Cohen, Donald A. Cook, Joe H. Harless, Ivan S. Horabin, Claude S. Lineberry, Stuart Margulies, Francis Mechner, Sif Wiksten, and Vivian Wilson.

In addition, my thinking has been profoundly influenced by the work of Thomas F. Gilbert and B.F. Skinner.

DEDICATION

To Vivian Wilson . . . a friend in need is a friend in deed.

D.H.B.

CONTENTS

ABSTRACT

PROGRAMMED INSTRUCTION

Programmed instruction is described as instructional packages having certain key characteristics or features: self-pacing; frequent opportunities for overt responding to problems/questions (items) accompanied by immediate feedback; and a highly-structured (programmed) sequence of self-instructional units (known historically as "frames"). The printed programmed text typifies such packages.

The programmed nature of PI instruction is described with reference to certain basic concepts concerning the organization or structure and intended functions of frame sequences and the frames within them:

- *Testing stimuli*—test items that call for overt (usually written) responses and typically are accompanied by some form of feedback by which the learner can evaluate the adequacy of her/his responses. These items appear in pre- and posttests, prerequisite tests, and frame sequences designed to teach the skills/knowledge specified by end-of-program objectives.

- *Teaching stimuli*—which can include any form of information that is judged effective and efficient for enabling the learners to develop the skills/knowledge tested by the items, such as directions and models of their application, definitions and examples, demonstrations—actual or simulated, etc.

- *Frame sequences*—in which teaching and testing stimuli are combined to form *initial teaching* (information plus items),

xi

intermediate teaching (reduced information plus more items), and *testing* (items alone without any teaching help) frames.

A general strategy for the design of frame sequences is examined:

- *Preview*—to provide an overview of and rationale for the frame sequence (the what and why of it).

- *Diagnostic-branching*—to provide both a *criterion pretest* (so that learner can skip the sequence if he/she has already learned what it teaches) and *prerequisite test* (to ensure that the learner brings to the sequence the skills/knowledge needed to benefit from the sequence).

- *Organizing set/theory*—to ensure that the learner enters the teaching-testing section with suitable "attending" behaviors for focusing on the critical teaching stimuli.

- *Teaching-testing*—initial and intermediate teaching and testing frames as mentioned above.

- *Practice*—to provide both *isolated practice* (more testing) of the skills/knowledge just learned plus *integrated practice* in which it is combined with previously learned behaviors.

Various specific strategies for programming the teaching-testing section are described.

The importance of empirical testing of programmed instruction to identify and eliminate faults in it and to ensure its validity as an instructional package is discussed.

A step-by-step guide for developing programmed instruction packages is presented.

Additional material concerns present day uses of PI and limitations.

PROGRAMMED INSTRUCTION

I.

INTRODUCTION

The term *programmed instruction* has acquired various meanings since its inception in the late 1950's. Generally, it has come to mean either or both of two things:

- A PROCESS for developing instruction systematically, starting with "behavioral objectives" and using tryouts of the instruction to make sure that it works satisfactorily.

- A PRODUCT (i.e., instructional package) having certain key features, such as a highly structured (programmed) sequence of instructional units (historically called "frames") with frequent opportunities for the learner to respond via problems, questions, etc., typically accompanied by immediate feedback. The "programmed text" is typical of this kind of instructional package.

For purposes of this book, I will use a *product* definition of programmed instruction. However, in the Development Guide section of the book, I will describe an idealized *process* for creating such products.

This book has the following sections:

- INTRODUCTION–definition of programmed instruction (PI).

- USE–appropriate conditions and situations for the use of PI and some limitations thereon.

- OPERATIONAL DESCRIPTION—expansion of the definition, with emphasis on how programmed instruction works as illustrated by some samples of PI.

- DESIGN FORMAT—discussion of the overall structure of a PI package.

- OUTCOMES—the potential benefits of PI to learners and teachers (instructional programmers), particularly the aspects of testing PI to ensure that it works and the resulting "guaranteed" learning.

- DEVELOPMENT GUIDE—step-by-step description of a general, idealized model for creating programmed instruction.

- RESOURCES—where to go for additional information about PI.

- CONCLUDING COMMENTS—on the current and future status of PI.

- APPENDICES—samples of programmed frame sequences (exercises, lessons) in programmed text format.

A Definition of Programmed Instruction

As a *product*, programmed instruction or PI means to me an instructional package which has the characteristics or features identified in Tables 1 and 2.

For the information in Tables 1 and 2 to be really meaningful, I recommend that at this point you examine the two sample "programs" in the Appendices by reading through them and perhaps even responding to them as though you were a learner by writing your answers to the questions (items) in them.

Table 3 compares PI (as defined in Tables 1 and 2) with some alternate forms of instruction with respect to the specific characteristics/features stated in Table 1.

Table 1

Definition of PI Characteristics/Features

CHARACTERISTIC/FEATURE	QUALIFYING REMARKS
Mediated/Replicable • MEDIATED in the sense that the PI package involves print or nonprint media or a combination of these. • REPLICABLE in the sense that because it is mediated, the PI can be used repeatedly and still yield the same learning outcomes.	Technically, PI can be "mediated" by an instructor, but this special case (e.g., programmed lecture) will not be covered in this book.
Self-Administrable, Self-Paced • SELF-ADMINISTRABLE in the sense that the learner can do the basic instructional activities without frequent reliance on a "teacher." • SELF-PACED in that because it is self-administrable, the learner can work through the PI at a pace or rate determined by him/her.	The self-administrable feature does *not* rule out an instructor being present to distribute the materials, give directions, answer questions, score performance on criterion tests, conduct question-and-answer discussions, etc.
Frequent Overt Response Opportunities • By OVERT RESPONSE OPPORTUNITY I mean a specific item (problem, question, etc.) that calls for an overt learner response (oral, psychomotor, written). By FREQUENT I mean that the learner is responding to such items much of the time during the administration of PI.	The issue of overt versus covert (mental) responses has been studied in many investigations which, in my judgment, show that overt responses are preferable.
Immediate Feedback • IMMEDIATE FEEDBACK means that as soon as the	Feedback has been studied in many investigations which, in

Table 1 (Continued)

learner has responded to an item, he/she can then access some form of information with which to evaluate the adequacy of the responses just made. Feedback for responses to criterion tests may be controlled by the instructor.

my judgment, show both that it is important to facilitate learning and that "peeking" at the feedback prior to responding should be minimized.

Highly Structured (Programmed) Sequences

• PROGRAMMED means that the instruction provides branching or linear sequences of instructional units (frames) designed to control the learner's behavior in responding to the PI.

See Table 2 for explanation.

Table 2

Functional Parts of a PI
Frame Sequence (Exercise, Lesson)

INTRODUCTION (PREVIEW)	An overview or preview stating WHAT is to be learned and WHY it matters to the learner; may specify the frame sequence objective(s) behaviorally (so-called "behavioral objectives").
DIAGNOSTIC-BRANCHING SECTION (Optional)	• *Criterion pretest*—items testing the skills/knowledge taught; enables learner to by-pass or skip the frame sequence; optional. • *Prerequisites*—some means for reviewing or testing whether the learner has the entry skills/knowledge judged as prerequisite for learning from the frame sequence; optional.
ORGANIZING SET/THEORY SECTION (Optional)	Information intended to help the learner to focus on the critical elements in the teaching-testing section below; to establish the key *attending* or *observing* responses needed to process the teaching information or stimuli effectively; may include items; this optional section often done as part of the introduction.
TEACHING-TESTING SECTION	Frames intended to actually teach the skills/knowledge (criterion behavior) specified by the objective(s) for the frame sequence. • *Initial teaching*—one or more frames containing sufficient teaching information/stimuli to enable the learner to respond correctly to items that test for the skills/knowledge specified by the objective(s); the teaching information/stimuli may be in any form judged suitable for evoking the desired responses to the items (e.g., actual or filmed/videotaped demonstrations, visual depictions-drawings/photographs, sets of directions, samples of stimuli to be discriminated, explanatory material, etc.). Synonyms: *prime* or *priming* (Harless, Skinner), *demonstrate* (Gilbert).

Table 2 (Continued)

- *Intermediate teaching*—one or more frames in which the amount of teaching information/stimuli is reduced from that used in the initial teaching, and additional items are used to evoke the same basic skills/knowledge initiated in the initial teaching items; intermediate teaching is optional and can involve two or more frames with variations in the amount and nature of the teaching stimuli provided; often includes special test items. Synonym: *prompt* or *prompting* (Gilbert, Harless, Skinner).
- *Testing*—one or more frames in which all teaching information/stimuli are eliminated and the items test for the learner's acquisition of the skills/knowledge supposedly taught by the initial and intermediate teaching frames (i.e., the behavior specified by the objective(s) for the frame sequence). Synonyms: *perform* (Harless), *release* (Gilbert).

PRACTICE
SECTION

- *Isolated*—additional testing of the skills/knowledge with more complex/difficult items.
- *Integrated*—items testing and providing opportunities for combining the skills/knowledge just learned with those learned from prior frame sequences.

REVIEW/
SUMMARY
SECTION

Practice frames may be preceded or followed by a review or summary of either what was taught in this frame sequence (or everything taught so far in the PI program).

Table 3

Comparison of PI with Other Methods of Instruction

CHARACTERISTIC OR FEATURE	PI	ALTERNATE METHODS				
		AV SHOW	LAP	CLP	TEXT-BOOK	LECTURE
MEDIATED/ REPLICABLE	X	X	X	X	X	?
SELF-ADMINIS./ SELF-PACED	X	?	X		X	
FREQUENT RESPONSE ITEMS	X	?	?	?		
IMMEDIATE FEEDBACK	X	?	?	X		
PROGRAMMED SEQUENCES	X	?				

Notes

1. AV SHOW means any audio/visual presentation (e.g., sound-slide, videotape, etc.). If it includes frequent responding with feedback, then it should probably be considered an A/V form of PI.
2. LAP means Learning Activity Package, typically a printed set of directions for self-directed learning activities (e.g., objectives, resources, recommended activities, evaluation criteria/procedures), such as those used in Personalized Systems of Instruction (PSI)—the "Keller method." A LAP may include use of PI as a resource.
3. CLP means Construct Lesson Plan, as described by Langdon (1978).
4. TEXTBOOK means the standard, traditional textbook, including those with end-of-chapter quizzes. It does *not* include workbooks having frequent items and feedback for use in practicing skills.
5. LECTURE means the typical "stand-up" didactic presentation. It may be mediated/replicable to the extent given from a lesson guide

Table 3 (Continued)

or plan and supported by printed handouts, visuals, etc. But if it includes frequent items with feedback (whatever their form), it should be considered a PI-lecture. Here I am assuming the conventional lecture where the lecturer talks, occasionally asks questions, and responds to comments/questions as appropriate.

6. The table does not include "teaching machines," which I define as computerized or electro-mechanical devices for presenting PI. I include these under PI above.

Basic Assumptions

While we can deal with PI as a *product*—an instructional package having the characteristics/features discussed above—it would be misleading to do so without giving due attention to the *process* by which PI is created (see the Developmental Guide section for a step-by-step development model).

Consideration of the development process is essential because it determines the *quality* of the PI product as measured by the learning outcomes (see the Outcomes section).

When I discuss PI in the subsequent sections of this book, I make certain assumptions about the process by which the PI has been developed—that it includes the following basic ingredients.

(1) There has been an analysis of the need for PI—what some call *training needs assessment*—that shows it is reasonable to assume the following to be "true":

- Actual or anticipated *performance deficiencies* can be attributed to *skills/knowledge deficits*—that is, without some form of instruction or job aids the performers in question will not be able to do their jobs satisfactorily because they lack needed skills/knowledge.

- The appropriate intervention or remedy to correct or prevent these actual/anticipated performance deficiencies is *instruction for later recall* rather than the use of job aids to guide the desired (mastery) performance on the job.

(2) There has been an analysis of the comparative pros and cons of PI versus other forms of instruction that justifies PI as the optimum method from a "cost-effectiveness" viewpoint.

(3) There has been an analysis of the desired mastery performance—often called *task analysis*—which can be used as the basis for deriving the instructional objectives to be met via the PI.

Additionally, I am assuming that the PI product has been developed via a process that includes the steps described in the Developmental Guide section of this book, particularly some effort to actually test the PI through tryouts with learners representative of the target audience for whom the PI is intended.

References
(INTRODUCTION section)

Gilbert, T.F. Mathetics: II. The Design of Teaching Exercises. *Journal of Mathetics*, 1962, Vol. 2.

Harless, J.H. *Analysis and Instructional Design Workshop*. McLean, Va.: Harless Performance Guild, Inc., 1976.

Langdon, D.G. *The Construct Lesson Plan*. Englewood Cliffs, N.J.: Educational Technology Publications, 1978.

Skinner, B.F. *The Technology of Teaching*. New York: Appleton-Century-Crofts, 1968.

II.

USE

In discussing the use of PI, I will consider these aspects:

- *General* when-to-use considerations—already covered (see Basic Assumptions, in the previous chapter).

- *Specific* when-to-use considerations—which come in to play if the general considerations are favorable.

- *Illustrative applications*—use of PI for different purposes and so-called "teaching machines."

- *Limitations* on the use of PI.

Specific When-to-Use Considerations

There are no "hard-and-fast" rules for deciding when to use PI rather than some other form of instructional design. There are factors worth considering, however, such as the following:

- A relatively HIGH LEVEL OF RECALL must be produced by the instruction. PI can provide the kind of systematic "over-learning" practice needed to ensure later recall.

- SHAPING of specific behaviors and substantial PRACTICE of these behaviors (both isolated and then integrated practice) is needed to ensure effective, efficient acquisitions of the discriminations and generalizations, response chains or se-

13

quences, psychomotor proficiency, and/or rote associations involved in the skills/knowledge to be learned. PI provides the detailed structure needed for such shaping and practice.

- CAREFUL ATTENDING to the details of information/stimuli is needed to develop the desired skills/knowledge. PI can provide the closely controlled attending/observing responses required.

- ACTIVE PROCESSING (versus passive reading) of information is desired, even where there may be no real need for a high level of recall nor any real shaping and practice (for example, familiarizing employees with the organization). The PI format with its response items and feedback offers one suitable means for achieving such familiarization or orientation.

The factors above concern the learning process. There are also "administrative" considerations that can affect the decision to use PI. For example:

- VALIDATED INSTRUCTION is necessary to ensure consistent quality of outcomes independent of variations in instructors/instructional settings. Validated instruction means instruction that has been shown through tests or tryouts of it to enable the target audience learners to achieve at least a specified minimum amount of learning (e.g., 90 percent or better). To achieve such high quality of learned performance consistently, it is essential (I believe) to have instruction which incorporates the characteristics/features identified earlier (Tables 1 and 2). Thus, whenever there is a requirement for consistently high quality of learning through validated instruction, PI must be considered (see the section OUTCOMES for further discussion of empirical testing of PI).

- DE-CENTRALIZED, INDIVIDUALIZED, INSTRUCTOR-FREE INSTRUCTION is desirable or necessary. PI is an obvious method to consider whenever the instruction must be *de-centralized* (i.e., cannot be administered to groups due to cost, geographic location, and/or scheduling problems), must be *individualized* (i.e., permit self-administration/self-pacing), and/or must be *instructor-free* (i.e., practical constraints rule out the use of instructors except as "administrators" or "managers").

Illustrative Applications

At present one can find various kinds of applications of PI. Some of the more typical are described below to give you a "feel" for current uses of PI as an instructional design.

- SELF-CONTAINED "TOPIC" INSTRUCTION—where a particular subject matter or topic is taught and stands more-or-less by itself. The library of programmed texts published by John Wiley & Sons under the direction of Judith Vantrease Wilson offers a number of good examples (e.g., "Clear Writing," "Ecology," "Study Skills," "Thinking Metric," etc.). In business/industry, an example is the product knowledge PI texts used for Sales Rep training by Lanier Business Products.

- SUPPLEMENTAL INSTRUCTION—where a course or workshop has PI material as a supplement to the main instructional activities. For example, Harless' *Ounce of Analysis* PI text is mailed out to workshop participants as a pre-workshop assignment to give an overview of the basic concepts in his workshop on "Performance Problem-Solving." PI packages may be used as "enrichment" or for remedial instruction in connection with a course.

- COMPONENT OF INSTRUCTION—where a course or workshop uses PI units as part of the main instructional activities. For example, in a graduate course in programmed instruction, I used Bullock and Wilson's *Analyzing Self-Instructional Programs* and their *Editing/Revising Self-Instructional Programs* (both of which are PI texts plus reference materials) to teach key skills/knowledge. Homme and Tosti's *Behavior Technology* is another example of PI designed for use as an actual component of a course concerned with behavior modification and contingency management. In the Harless Performance Guild's various workshops, PI exercises or lessons (often called "dialogues") are integral components.

- JOB AID FAMILIARIZATION AND USE—an increasingly

common use of PI is to familiarize learners with and to teach
them the use of job aids (e.g., checklists, decision tables,
flowcharts, worksheets, etc., actually used on the job to guide
the desired performance). Typically the objective of the PI is
to enable the learner to apply the job aids on the job. For
example, in training Bell System personnel to use the codes
involved in a new functional accounting system, the basic
instructional "tool" is a booklet containing various job aids for
coders to use when coding on the job. The use of this job aids
booklet is taught by a set of PI lesson booklets, one for each
type of code. In sales training, Lineberry working with the
Bank of America developed PI lessons for use in a workshop
designed to teach the use of various job aids in selling various
bank services. One of these programs includes programmed
role-playing scripts with videotape feedback.

The kinds of applications of PI described above represent,
in my experience, the major current uses of PI.

**Programmed Instruction and
"Teaching Machines"**

In the early days of programmed instruction (late 1950's,
early 1960's) there was a flurry of interest in "teaching
machines," and a number of devices were marketed commercially. The "revolution" these "auto-instructional" devices
were supposed to help bring about in education and training
failed to materialize, for reasons that need not concern us
here.

But, while most if not all of these early teaching machines
are no longer with us, except as antique relics of a bygone
era, the concept has certainly lived on. Teaching machines
continue to be of interest because of certain key advantages
they offer in contrast with the programmed text:

- MECHANIZED RESPONDING via keyboards, pushbutton,
  etc.—which makes possible automatic recording and scoring of
  response and selective feedback based on the nature of the
  learner's response to an item.

• AUTOMATED CONTROL of teaching stimuli—which makes possible sophisticated branching and optional prompting based on learner responses, plus elimination of "peeking" at feedback prior to responding and requirement for learners to correct their errors before preceding further. Domenech (1974) has shown the latter to facilitate learning of detailed responses (spelling medical terms).

At present the most challenging and potentially significant teaching machine is the computer. Substantial advances have been made since its early use, when it served mainly as an expensive "fancy page-turner." Projects such as PLATO and TICCIT illustrate effective use of the computer, but cost factors are still too high to make feasible comprehensive use of the computer other than in specialized circumstances.

Other teaching machines currently available are specially-designed audiovisual devices which provide for keyboard/pushbutton responding. Discussion of these is beyond the scope of this book.

To the instructional programmer, the important thing to keep in mind about teaching machines, whatever their form, is that the PI they provide reflects the same basic concepts that characterize the programmed text as described in this book. That is, the programming of instruction and PI packages involve, in my opinion, the same basic functional parts and relationships, regardless of the particular delivery mechanism—printed text or automated device.

Limitations on the Use of PI

To discuss meaningfully the limitations on the use of PI, it helps, I find, to begin with the self-contained (no instructor) programmed text and the optimum conditions for its effective use. The most important optimum conditions seem to me to be the following:

- The learners have *adequate reading skills* for learning from self-instruction.

- The learners are *able to follow directions*—to read and think about the teaching stimuli, to respond as called for by the testing stimuli (items), to access the feedback, to go on to the next frame, etc.

- The learners can *self-evaluate their responses* on the basis of the feedback information/stimuli.

In this context, limitations on the use of PI can be considered with respect to deviations from these optimum conditions and possible means for solving problems that arise when these optimum conditions aren't present.

Reading-Skills Limitations

Suppose the learners cannot read. We can attempt to use audio inputs instead of print. The same applies if the learners have limited reading skills.

Obviously, the use of audio inputs in such situations won't work if the skills/knowledge to be learned involve printed information. Still, deficient or non-readers could be taught via PI various skills/knowledge, such as discriminations of visual stimuli (e.g., naming letters and numerals orally), other speech behaviors, psychomotor skills (e.g., using tools), and so on.

Following-Directions Limitations

Suppose the learners cannot follow directions as required to do the things involved in PI learning; for example, pre-schoolers. We can attempt to have the directions stated orally and demonstrated by a teacher who monitors the learner's performance to make sure the directions are followed.

Using Feedback for Self-Evaluation Limitations

Effective learning from PI depends critically on the learner being able to use the immediate feedback to self-evaluate the adequacy of her/his responses to the items in the program. Among the factors that can interfere with self-evaluation from immediate feedback are the following:

- The learners lack the necessary skill/knowledge to self-evaluate their responses because they are "too young." For example, they are unable to "match" their responses with the feedback stimuli, perhaps because they cannot follow the directions involved. Possible solutions for this kind of problem include:

    —Having a teacher provide suitable feedback.
    —Using a special form of feedback, such as the "invisible ink" developed by New Century Publications (e.g., the learner rubs with a special marker which reveals the feedback) or the use of a teaching machine that generates suitable feedback for pushbutton responding.

- The learners cannot self-evaluate their responses because the behavior involved is of such nature (e.g., too complex) to permit self-evaluation. Possible solutions for this kind of problem include:

    —Having a qualified observer provide immediate feedback.
    —Having the responses audio- or videotaped, after which the learner interacts with a qualified evaluator and obtains feedback by this means.

Another approach that can work is to first teach with PI the self-evaluation skills/knowledge needed to self-evaluate complex behaviors and then to have the learner use these self-evaluation skills/knowledge to self-evaluate her/his responses (which could include self-evaluating audio/video-recorded behaviors made during the PI); for example, learning to discriminate between aggressive and assertive behavior before learning to be assertive.

References
(USE section)

Bullock, D.H. and V. Wilson. *Analyzing Self-Instructional Programs*. Columbia, Md.: Behavioral Design Associates, Inc., 1974.

Bullock, D.H. and V. Wilson. *Editing/Revising Programs for Self-Instruction*. Columbia, Md.: Behavioral Design Associates, Inc., 1974.

Domenech, O. The Comparative Effectiveness of Flagged, Non-Flagged, and Forced-Correction of Errors in Computer-Assisted Programmed Learning. Unpublished Doctoral Dissertation, Catholic University, 1974.

Ellson, D.G., L. Barber, T.L. Engle and T. Kampwerth. Programmed Tutoring: A Teaching Aid and a Research Tool. *Reading Research Quarterly*, 1965, *1*, 77-127.

Harless, J.H. *Ounce of Analysis*. McLean, Va.: Harless Performance Guild, Inc., 1975.

Homme, L. and D. Tosti. *Behavior Technology*. San Rafael, California: Individual Learning Systems, Inc., 1971.

III.

OPERATIONAL DESCRIPTION

Let's begin the operational description of PI by examining a sample frame sequence (exercise, lesson), "Calculating Batting Averages," which can be found at the back of the book (Appendix A).

Sample Frame Sequence
This sample frame sequence illustrates the functional parts of a PI frame sequence described in Table 2. Below I have discussed each frame with respect to its intended instructional *function*.

Frame 1—Introduction
This frame provides an introduction or preview for the frame sequence. It states WHAT is to be learned (calculating batting averages) and WHY this matters to the learner (keeping track of one's hitting).

*Frame 2—Diagnostic-Branching Section**
This frame provides a CRITERION PRETEST. It tests the

---

*Frames 2, 3, and 4 each direct the learner to have the coach score the test performances. The assumption is that Little Leaguers may be unable to determine adequately without help whether they can already calculate batting averages or have the needed prerequisite skills/knowledge. Actually, I have included this feature mainly to illustrate how an instructor can be involved in evaluating and giving feedback on certain frames in a PI program.

same behavior taught by the later frames in the teaching-testing section (Frames 6-9). Its function is to enable the learner to by-pass or skip the frame sequence if the behavior it teaches has already been learned elsewhere.

*Frame 3—Diagnostic-Branching Section**

This frame provides a PREREQUISITE TEST. Its function is to test for certain entry skills/knowledge the learner must already have learned in order to benefit from the subsequent frames—counting official times at bat. If the learner fails this prerequisite test, then some form of remedial instruction is indicated before proceeding further (e.g., reviewing the self-instructional program "Official Times at Bat" listed on the cover).

*Frame 4—Diagnostic-Branching Section**

This frame provides another PREREQUISITE TEST. Its function is to test for additional entry skills/knowledge needed to learn from the later teaching-testing frames—doing long division with decimals. Here, too, if the learner fails this test some form of remedial instruction is indicated (e.g., reviewing the self-instructional program "Doing Long Division with Decimal Points" also listed on the cover).

Frame 5—Organizing Set/Theory Section

This function intended for this frame is to give the learner an idea of the key things to pay attention to in the teaching frames that follow. I don't offer this as a particularly good example, and have included it mainly to illustrate the concept. Test items could have been added, if desired. For example:

- If your batting average were .200, we would say that you are batting . . . .

- If you were batting four hundred, this would be shown as . . . .

Frame 6—Teaching-Testing Section

This is the first of four teaching-testing frames (Frames 6-9) designed to actually teach the criterion behavior of calculating batting averages. The intended function of this frame is INITIAL TEACHING (which Gilbert calls "demonstrate" and Harless and Skinner call "prime" or "priming"). The basic aim here is to initiate the behavior to be learned through a combination of:

- Sufficient teaching information/stimuli to enable the learner to do the basic calculation—an *algorithm* (set of directions stating the steps involved) plus a *model* (an example of the application of the algorithm to specific data).

- A test item (testing stimulus) requiring the learner to calculate a batting average by applying the teaching information.

Note that in Frame 6—as distinguished from Frames 7-9—special teaching help is provided by setting up the calculation in long division format.

Frame 7—Teaching-Testing Section Continued

This is the second of the four frames of the teaching-testing section. Two key functions are present:

- There are two special items that serve an observing function—paying attention to the elements official times at bat and hits—by reviewing the prerequisite skills/knowledge tested in Frame 3.

- Teaching information/stimuli are combined with a test item, as in Frame 6, so that the learner once again calculates a batting average—only this time with *less* teaching help than in Frame 6. Only the algorithm is given and it is stated as a rule rather than as a series of steps; no model is provided.

Note that Frame 7 includes reminders about the decimal point which are dropped in Frames 8-9.

Frame 7 has as its main function INTERMEDIATE TEACHING (which Gilbert, Harless, and Skinner all refer to as "prompting"). The primary difference between Frame 6 (initial teaching or priming) and Frame 7 (intermediate teaching or prompting) lies in their teaching information/stimuli: *Frame 7 has a reduction in the amount of teaching help provided*, while at the same time testing for the same behavior of calculating a batting average.

Frame 8—Teaching-Testing Section Continued

This frame also has an intermediate or prompting function. The difference between Frames 7 and 8 is this: in Frame 7 the teaching information/stimuli are in the form of an algorithm without a model, whereas in Frame 8 there is a model without an algorithm. Both have items calling for calculating a batting average.

Frame 9—Teaching-Testing Section Continued

Here for the first time the behavior of calculating a batting average is tested in the absence of any teaching information or stimuli. The function is evaluation or TESTING (which Gilbert calls "release" and Harless "perform").

Table 4 shows the structure of the teaching-testing section (Frames 6-9) of this sample frame sequence.

For purposes of ISOLATED PRACTICE, Frame 9 could contain additional criterion test items or it could be followed by additional testing frames.

Frame 10—Integrated Practice

Once the behavior of calculating batting averages has been taught in the teaching-testing frames, there may be a need or opportunity for what is identified in Table 2 as

Table 4

The Structure of Frames 6-9,
Calculating Batting Averages

	FRAME 6	FRAME 7	FRAME 8	FRAME 9
BASIC FUNCTION	initial teaching	intermediate teaching	intermediate teaching	testing
SYNONYMS	demonstrate, prime	prompt	prompt	release, perform
FUNCTION DEFINED	to initiate the criterion behavior for the frame sequence	to strengthen the criterion behavior via reductions in teaching stimuli	as in Frame 7	to test for acquisition of the criterion behavior
METHOD				
• Teaching stimuli	algorithm plus model	algorithm without model	model without algorithm	none
• Special teaching stimuli	long division format with labels	decimal point reminders		
• Testing stimuli (items)	test item for criterion behavior	test items for criterion behavior	test item for criterion behavior	test item for criterion behavior
• Special testing stimuli (items)		prerequisite review items		

INTEGRATED PRACTICE. For example, as noted in Frame 10, the just-learned behavior of calculating batting averages could now be integrated with the previously-learned behavior of interpreting a scorecard.

Another Sample Frame Sequence

Let's examine now another sample frame sequence (exercise, lesson), "Classifying Quadrilaterals" (Appendix B).

As did the "Calculating Batting Averages" program, the sample frame sequence in Appendix B illustrates the functional parts of PI frame sequences described in Table 2. For purposes of this book, these two samples of PI are parallel in most key respects to emphasize how two *different behaviors*—calculating a batting average (which is a response chain) and classifying quadrilaterals (which involves discriminations and generalizations)—can be taught using the *same basic, general PI strateggy.*

Frame 1—Introduction
Provides a *preview* stating the WHAT and WHY of the frame sequence and relating it to the previous frame sequence.

Frame 2—Diagnostic-Branching Section
Provides a *criterion* pretest for the frame sequence.

Frame 3—Diagnostic-Branching Section
Provides a *prerequisites review test.*

Frame 4—Diagnostic-Branching Section
Provides an additional *prerequisites review test.*

Frame 5—Organizing Set/Theory
Intended to provide an idea of the basic things to attend to

or keep in mind during the teaching-testing frames that follow and includes some hopefully amusing "mnemonics" that may help the learner with the initial learning. This frame could have included items designed to strengthen the mnemonics.

Frame 6—Teaching-Testing Section
Provides the *initial teaching* (demonstrate, prime) function—teaching information/stimuli in the form of definitions and examples of the four concepts to be learned plus test items that call for classifying of new figures on the basis of the definitions and examples. The mnemonics are repeated.

> NOTE: In the "Calculating Batting Averages" sample, the teaching information/stimuli were in the form of algorithms and models, whereas here definitions and examples are used. The basis for choosing between such different teaching information/stimuli is discussed later.

Frame 7—Teaching-Testing Section
Provides the *intermediate teaching* (prompting) function, using examples of the stimuli to be discriminated without definitions. Note that there are some special items at the start designed to evoke attending/observing responses focussed on key features and comparisons. The final test item requires the same classifying behavior as in Frame 6.

Frame 8—Teaching-Testing Section
Provides additional *intermediate teaching* (prompting), this time using the definitions without examples plus items that call for the same classifying behavior as in Frames 6-7.

Frame 9—Teaching-Testing Section
Provides the *testing* (perform, release) function. Items

requiring the same classifying behavior as in Frames 6-8 appear without any teaching information/stimuli. For purposes of ISOLATED PRACTICE, Frame 9 might be followed by a series of frames testing further the classifying behavior.

Frame 10—Integrated Practice
Now that the concepts of rhomboid, rhombus, trapezium, and trapezoid have been taught and tested, they are combined with concepts from the previous lesson.

Further Analysis of Teaching
and Testing Stimuli
We have examined frame-by-frame two sample frame sequences. Each illustrates the highly-structured (programmed) organization of PI described earlier in Table 2. Furthermore, taken together they illustrate how the basic instructional strategy described in Table 2 can be reflected in different teaching and testing stimuli for self-instruction of different behaviors.

Because these two components—teaching and testing stimuli—are so fundamental to PI, let's examine them further.

Testing Stimuli—Items
First let's examine the basic structure of teaching stimuli (items), which are used to provide opportunities for overt learner responses in the prerequisite, teaching-testing, and practice sections of frame sequences. As illustrated below, testing stimuli or items have three basic components: the INPUT STIMULUS, the RESPONSE MECHANISM, and the FEEDBACK.

Note that the feedback below assumes that the learner can distinguish alternate acceptable and non-acceptable answers.

SAMPLE ITEM A

Which cause(s) of performance deficiencies support considering job aids
as a remedy or solution? ....
....

INPUT STIMULUS—in this
case a direct question.

RESPONSE MECHANISM—
blank (with the implied direction to write an answer
there).

—————————
FEEDBACK: Skill/knowledge deficit,
or S/K (or an equivalent answer).

FEEDBACK—correct answers
plus a qualifying comment.

SAMPLE ITEM B

[DRAWINGS OF SIMPLE ELECTRI-
CAL CIRCUITS IDENTIFIED BY
LETTERS. SOME ARE PARALLEL,
THE OTHERS ARE SERIES CIR-
CUITS.]

INPUT STIMULUS—drawings
to be discriminated.

CIRCLE below the letters that identify parallel circuits above:

RESPONSE MECHANISM—
directions for how to respond
and letters to circle/not
circle.

[LETTERS TO CIRCLE OR NOT
CIRCLE.]

—————————
FEEDBACK: [LETTERS IDENTIFY-
ING PARALLEL CIRCUITS IN THE
DRAWINGS ABOVE.]

FEEDBACK—correct letters
to circle.

Sample Item A above is an example of a CON-
STRUCTED-RESPONSE item—it requires the learner to
"construct" the answer or response. Sample Item B is an
example of a MULTIPLE CHOICE item—it requires the
learner to "choose" the answer(s). Generally, constructed-
response are used to test for RECALL, multiple-choice for

RECOGNITION (but it's not always that simple, as we'll discuss later).

Either constructed-response or multiple-choice items can have a wide diversity of INPUT STIMULI; for example:

- AUDITORY/VISUAL (or other) stimuli to which the learner must respond, such as:
  —Audio-recorded heart sound patterns (abnormal/normal)
  —Visual electrocardiograph recordings (abnormal/normal)
  —Audio-visual depiction of a device operating (functioning/malfunctioning).
  —Depictions of audio/visual stimuli (e.g., drawing or model or photograph of an engine, etc.)

- INFORMATIONAL stimuli to which the learner must respond, such as:
  —Data in the form of charts, graphs, tables, etc.
  —Information in the form of articles, letters/memos, reports, etc. (or excerpts from or summaries of same)
  —Job aids (or sections of)—checklists, decision tables, flowcharts, worksheets, etc.

- SOCIAL stimuli to which the learner must respond, such as:
  —Audio/video-taped (or filmed) depictions of actual or hypothetical social interaction situations
  —Descriptions of social interactions (e.g., printed script of an actual/hypothetical conversation, interview, telephone conversation, etc.)
  Role-playing situations simulating specific social interactions.

- Problems to solve/questions to answer, sometimes direct but often with reference to the kinds of input stimuli listed above.

By their very nature, constructed-response and multiple-choice items differ with respect to their RESPONSE MECHANISMS.

- CONSTRUCTED-RESPONSE item response mechanisms can include such things as:

—*Directions* to perform specified actions—build something, given the needed materials; draw diagrams; manipulate the controls of some device/equipment; perform a laboratory experiment; etc. (where psychomotor actions are called for, there is usually some tangible output involved as the basis for feedback—recording the result, videotape of complex actions, etc.)
—*Entries* to be made in charts, graphs, tables, worksheets, etc.
—*Questions* followed by blanks or open space
—*Sentences* with one or more words replaced by blanks (generally not recommended).

It must be emphasized that *criterion* test items in constructed-response form can call for quite complex behaviors involving combinations of skills/knowledge learned previously from the PI. For example, analyze and make decisions about a set of data/information (e.g., case problem, in-basket exercise); design a system, diagram it, and write explanatory notes based on a suitable set of input data/ information; write all or parts of a proposal or report from source data/information; and so on.

- MULTIPLE-CHOICE item response mechanisms can include such things as:
  —*Indicator* responses (e.g., checking, circling, underlining, writing X's), including psychomotor (e.g., pushing buttons)
  —*Grids or matrices* in which to enter checks, codes, X's, etc.
  —*Ordering or ranking* (e.g., writing numerals to show the order in which the choices listed normally occur)
  —*Matching* (e.g., two columns or lists of things to be matched)

While the distinction between constructed-response and multiple-choice items is important and useful, it must be realized that they may often be used in combinations. For example:

- Information presented, learner *chooses* the correct analysis or interpretation or solution (multiple-choice) and writes an explanation or justification of that choice (constructed-response).

- Or the learner states her/his solution (constructed-response) and chooses the category in which that solution belongs (multiple-choice).

Basically, constructed-response and multiple-choice items can provide the same kinds of FEEDBACK. The one real difference is where constructed-response items call for fairly complex behavior, such as a series of actions or responses.

For simpler responses to items, feedback can include:

- CORRECT ANSWERS OR RESPONSES—the desired answer or response is provided as feedback.

- PLUS COMMENTARY—the correct answer or response may be accompanied by commentary explaining why it is correct and/or why some alternative is incorrect.

- WITH ACCEPTABLE ALTERNATIVES—as appropriate, acceptable alternative answers or responses may be provided (or the feedback for constructed-response items may include a qualifier such as "or an equivalent answer").

For more complex constructed-response items, feedback can take such forms as:

- CHECKOFF CRITERIA—a list of criteria to be used for evaluating the responses, perhaps with check boxes to facilitate systematic evaluation.

- POSITIVE/NEGATIVE MODELS—models (examples) of acceptable and not acceptable responses may be provided, preferably with accompanying commentary explaining why they are/are not okay.

- OBSERVER CRITIQUE—an observer may be used to evaluate

the responses and to provide feedback in the form of a critique, preferably using checkoff criteria as noted above.

Functions of Testing Stimuli (Items)

We have just examined the structure of testing stimuli or items. In designing items for PI, we decide the CONTENT—the input stimuli, response mechanism, feedback—on the basis of the intended FUNCTION of the item. For example:

IF	THEN . . . .
The item is a *criterion item* to test for an end-of-program objective	The *content* should reflect the on-the-job task on which the objective is based.

Generally, the functions of items have to do with their relationship to the functional parts of a frame sequence (Table 2) as illustrated by the sample frame sequences examined earlier (Appendices A, B). Since the concept of CRITERION ITEM is critical to my discussion of item functions, let's start by making sure we understand the meaning of that term.

Suppose we have a PI program consisting of three frame sequences (exercises, lessons) having as the end-of-program objective the following three-step criterion behavior involved in performance problem-solving:

A. Specify performance deficiencies
B. Analyze their causes
C. Decide on cause-relevant remedies or solutions.

Let's assume that the PI program for teaching this behavior has this structure:

Frame Seq.	Intro./Preview	Diagnostic-Branching Crit T PreREQ		Teaching-Testing Section	Practice-Isolated	Practice-Integ'd	Criterion Posttest
(1)	A-B-C	A-B-C	A-B-C	A	A	---	---
(2)	B	---	---	B	B	A-B	---
(3)	C	---	---	C	C	A-B-C	A-B-C

Crit T   =   criterion pretest

PreREQ   =   prerequisites test

In relation to the three-frame sequence PI program depicted above, we can distinguish three "levels" of items:

- CRITERION ITEMS for end-of-program objectives — test the skills/knowledge or criterion behavior specified by the end-of-program objectives

- SUB-CRITERION ITEMS for sub-divisions of the end-of-program objectives — test parts of or simpler versions of the skills/knowledge or criterion behavior tested by criterion items

- OTHER/SPECIAL ITEMS for enabling objectives — test for specific aspects of the skills/knowledge or criterion behavior

To illustrate this three-level differentiation with respect to the three-frame sequence PI program depicted above:

- CRITERION ITEM—given a set of data/information, specify each indicated performance deficiency (A), analyze the likely cause(s) of each deficiency (B), and decide a cause-relevant remedy or solution for each deficiency (C). This criterion behavior is tested by criterion items in the criterion pretest (1), integrated practice (2), and criterion posttest (3).

- SUB-CRITERION ITEM—given data/information, specify the indicated performance deficiency—teaching-testing and isolated practice (1); OR given a specified performance deficiency and associated data/information, analyze the likely cause(s)—teaching-testing and isolated practice (2); OR given a performance deficiency and its likely cause(s), decide a cause-relevant remedy/solution—teaching-testing and isolated practice (3).

- OTHER/SPECIAL ITEMS—given statements specifying performance deficiencies, choose whether each statement is acceptable and, if not, choose the reason(s) why not—could appear as part of teaching (1); OR given statements of possible causes of a performance deficiency, classify each as stating a skill/knowledge deficit, environmental obstacle, or motivational factor—could appear as part of teaching (2); OR given a particular cause category, choose the appropriate class(es) of cause-relevant remedy/solution(s)—could appear as part of teaching (3).

PREREQUISITE items are usually either criterion/sub-criterion items from earlier frame sequences in the PI program, or they test skills/knowledge presumably learned elsewhere from some other pre-PI instruction.

The Content of Criterion/ Sub-Criterion Items

Ideally, the skills/knowledge or criterion behavior being tested by criterion/sub-criterion test items should reflect as directly as practically possible the on-the-job performance for which the learner is being prepared by the PI program. Thus, the input stimuli should be identical to or at least match reasonably well those encountered on the job; the response mechanisms should permit responses identical to or that at least match reasonably well the responses required on the job; and the feedback should approximate that likely to occur during on-the-job performance.

The idealized PI development process described in the Development Guide section of this book is designed to ensure that the CONTENT of criterion and sub-criterion items reflects the nature of the target on-the-job performance. These key steps are involved:

- TASK ANALYSIS—analyzing and specifying the desired on-the-job performance (mastery).

- OBJECTIVES SPECIFICATION—deriving end-of-program (terminal) objectives on the basis of the mastery performance specified in the task analysis.

- CRITERION TESTS—developing criterion tests (sets of items) that call for the skills/knowledge or criterion behavior specified by the end-of-program objectives.

- SUB-OBJECTIVES/SUB-CRITERION TESTS—deriving from the end-of-program objectives the sub-objectives for specific frame sequences and the sub-criterion items for these sub-objectives.

A grid or matrix like that on page 37 can be helpful in determining how closely end-of-program objectives and their criterion test items match the original on-the-job (OTJ) mastery performance specified by task analysis.

Other/Special Testing Stimuli (Items)

We have been examining the content (input stimuli, response mechanisms, feedback) of criterion, sub-criterion, and prerequisite test items. There are other items that may appear in PI frame sequence, usually within the initial and

	INPUT STIMULI	RESPONSE MECHANISM	FEEDBACK CRITERIA
MASTERY OTJ PERFORMANCE			
END-OF-PROGRAM OBJECTIVE(S)			
CRITERION TEST ITEM(S)			

intermediate teaching. These items—which I call OTHER/ SPECIAL TESTING STIMULI (ITEMS)—have the same structure as other testing stimuli or items, but differ in their TEACHING FUNCTIONS.

Generally, the teaching function of these other/special items is to evoke COVERT (mental) responses involved in and underlying the criterion behavior or skills/knowledge being taught by the frame sequence. Among the specific functions that can be served by other/special items are the following:

- ATTENDING/OBSERVING functions—to direct the attention of the learner to specific information/stimuli, such as key aspects or features of teaching stimuli, job aids, etc. For example:

READ THE NARRATIVE FOR CODE # 219

Notice the Cautions section.

What code does it tell you to consider as an alternative to Code # 219? _____

The function of this sample other/special item is to make sure that the learner attends to/observes the Cautions section of the Code Narratives.

———————

Code # 239.

- DISCRIMINATION/GENERALIZATION functions—to strengthen key covert responses involved in discriminations/ generalizations. For example:

1. What do the rhomboid and rhombus have in common?
   a. equilateral   □
   b. non-right-angled   □
2. How do they differ?
   a. rhomboid is equilateral, rhombus is not   □
   b. rhombus is equilateral, rhomboid is not.   □

— — — — — — — —
1. b
2. b

The function of this sample other/special item is to strengthen the learners discrimination between the rhomboid and rhombus (the latter is equilateral) and the generalization between them (both are non-right-angled). This item could have been used in the intermediate teaching part of Classifying Quadrilaterals (Appendix B).

- RESPONSE CHAINS/SEQUENCES functions . . . to strengthen the links between the responses making up a response chain or sequence. For example:

LIST the steps in calculating a batting average:

— — — — — — — —
1. Find times at bat (AB)
2. Find the number of hits (H)
3. Divide times at bat *into* the number of hits.

The function of this sample other/special item is to strengthen a covert response of remembering the steps for calculating batting averages. It could have been used in the intermediate teaching part of that sample frame sequence (Appendix A).

Other/special testing stimuli or items can, obviously, take a variety of forms, depending on their instructional function. Instructional programmers are tempted (in my experience) to become highly "creative" in their design and use of other/ special items. Nonetheless, I recommend this rule:

- AVOID using other/special items until you have data from testing (e.g., developmental tryouts) of the PI without them which shows they are needed.

- Stated another way, a basic programming strategy—sometimes called "lean programming"—is to restrict your teaching-testing section items to criterion/sub-criterion test items and only to go beyond that by adding other/special items IF data from your tests show these to be needed.

Enabling Objectives

The term ENABLING OBJECTIVES generally refers to either sub-criterion behavior and their sub-criterion items or to the skills/knowledge tested by other/special items. Discussion of enabling objectives and their associated test items is beyond the scope of this book.

Teaching Information/Stimuli

We have been examining the structure and functions of testing stimuli (items). Earlier we pointed out that in the initial and intermediate teaching parts of a frame sequence (the priming and prompting parts), we combine testing stimuli/items with TEACHING INFORMATION/STIMULI to initiate and strengthen the skills/knowledge or criterion behavior being taught by the frame sequence.

Teaching information/stimuli can take various forms:

- Actual or recorded DEMONSTRATIONS of the desired behavior or simulations depicting the input stimuli and resulting actions—these are good for teaching psychomotor and social interaction behaviors.

- DEFINITIONS and/or positive/negative EXAMPLES for teaching discriminations and generalizations—such as in the Classifying Quadrilaterals frame sequence (Appendix B).

- DIRECTIONS or RULES (e.g., algorithms) and MODELS of their application for teaching response chains or sequences— such as in the Calculating Batting Averages frame sequence (Appendix A).

Content and Function. As with testing stimuli/items, the CONTENT of teaching information/stimuli is decided primarily on the basis of the desired TEACHING FUNC-TION.

A crude, simple way to think about the design of teaching stimuli (one that I find helpful) goes something like this:

(1) For the learner to respond correctly to the criterion test items at the end of a frame sequence, the learner must acquire the necessary COVERT (mental) responses or "thoughts."

(2) The teaching information/stimuli used in initial and intermediate teaching must be designed, therefore, to "plant" the needed "thoughts" in the learner's "mind."

(3) A good way to figure out the covert (mental) responses needed—and thereby the teaching information/stimuli needed—is to analyze the criterion behavior or skills/knowledge called for by the criterion test items, using the following "rules."

If-Then "Rules" for Designing Teaching Information/Stimuli

IF the criterion test items call for. . . .	THEN consider using as teaching information/stimuli. . . .
(1) Discriminations/generalizations—classifying things, recognizing things, etc.	Definitions accompanied by positive/negative examples.
(2) Chains or sequences of responses to occur in particular order	Directions or rules (algorithms) accompanied by models showing the results of carrying out the directions/rules.
(3) Psychomotor or social interaction behavior—operating a device, selling skills, etc.	Demonstrations—actual, recorded, simulated—of the behavior in question.

Another similar way to think about the design of teaching information/stimuli and the initial and intermediate teaching parts is this:

(1) First design a "job aid" that will enable the learner to respond correctly to the criterion items for the frame sequence. The same if/then rules apply as shown above.

(2) Then figure out how to eliminate ("fade" or "vanish") the "job aid" through progressive elimination of its parts and/or simplifying it during the intermediate teaching (prompting).

Instructional (PI) Strategies

The design of PI frame sequences (exercises, lessons) can be based on what I will call INSTRUCTIONAL (or PI) STRATEGIES. Two kinds of strategies can be identified:

- BASIC, GENERAL STRATEGIES—like that described in Table 2, which resembles in most key respects those developed by Gilbert (1962) and Harless (1975). These are strategies that apply to the overall organization or structure of a PI frame sequence.

- SPECIFIC STRATEGIES—which apply essentially to the teaching-testing section within a basic, general strategy. These are strategies for the initial/intermediate teaching (priming and prompting) parts of a PI frame sequence.

Generally, specific PI strategies are designed to solve particular learning problems and take the form of combinations of teaching-testing stimuli for teaching the criterion behavior (skills/knowledge) specified by a specific objective.

- ALGORITHMIC STRATEGIES—for teaching response chains or sequences, as in the Calculating Batting Averages frame sequence (Appendix A), where a typical arrangement is:
  —Initial teaching (priming)   Algorithm plus model
  —Intermediate teaching   Algorithm alone, then
    (prompting)   model alone

where *algorithm* means the directions or rule for carrying out a chain or sequence of actions or responses and *model* means a sample of the result of applying the algorithm.

- DEFINITIONAL STRATEGIES—for teaching discriminations and generalizations, as in the Classifying Quadrilaterals frame sequence (Appendix B), where a typical arrangement is:
  —Initial teaching (priming)   Definitions plus examples
  —Intermediate teaching   Examples alone, then
  (prompting)   Definitions alone
  where *definition* means a statement of the defining characteristics, features, or properties of the stimuli to be discriminated or generalized and *examples* mean positive/negative instances.

- INDUCTIVE STRATEGIES—in which a particular way of thinking about a problem or process is taught "inductively," as in Harless' *Ounce of Analysis* (1975); beyond the scope of this book.

- INFORMATIONAL STRATEGIES—in which essentially "factual" information is communicated through the use of items designed to ensure active processing of the information in question; beyond the scope of this book.

- "SHAPING" STRATEGIES—in which complex, difficult criterion behavior is developed via a series of "successive approximations," each of which moves closer to the terminal skills/knowledge called for by the end-of-program objective. While this is also beyond the scope of this book, an example is that of learners acquiring the skills/knowledge needed to detect pathological signs in microscopic slides of "cells." The shaping strategy might involve:
  —Frame sequence with responding to simple drawings of "cells"
  —Frame sequence with responding to complex drawings
  —Frame sequence with responding to black-and-white photographs
  —Frame sequence with responding to color photographs
  —Criterion posttest with responding to slides viewed through a microscope (assumes that operating the microscope is prerequisite behavior).

Sequencing PI Objectives

I have deliberately avoided in the preceding discussion of the operational characteristics of PI the matter of the grouping and ordering of the end-of-program objectives and associated sub-objectives within a PI program—what I refer to as SEQUENCING.

In the Design Format section I have discussed the outline or table of contents of a complex and hypothetical PI program involving a number of end-of-program objectives and, therefore, a series of frame sequences (exercises, lessons) for these objectives.

Here I wish to discuss quite briefly the matter of arranging the end-of-program objectives/sub-objectives into a PI sequence which thus determines the sequence of frames making up the total PI program.

Quite briefly, because whereas proposed "rules" for sequencing of PI objectives are rampant (scratch an instructional programmer and you'll uncover a PI sequencing theorist!), there are few if any rules that can be defended on the basis of research findings. Nonetheless, as this is my book, I've taken here the liberty of suggesting certain sequencing "rules" I find worth considering when designing the sequence of objectives in a PI program.

- BACKWARD CHAINING—if the criterion behavior specified by an end-of-program objective involves a chain or sequence of actions or responses, it may be worthwhile considering what has been called "backward chaining" or "retrogressive chaining" (Alden, 1978). In backward chaining sequences, each step of the chain is taught in reverse order, starting with the last. For example, backward chaining of the performance problem-solving steps discussed previously, a backward chaining sequence would involve the following:

  —First, teach the step of deciding cause-relevant remedies or solutions, given specifications of performance deficiencies and analyses of their likely causes.

−Next, teach the step of analyzing likely causes of performance deficiencies and include integrated practice of this step with the step taught first.

−Then teach the first step, specifying performance deficiencies and move to integrated practice of all three steps and the criterion posttest.

In effect, three-frame sequences teaching C, then B-C, and finally A-B-C.

• FORWARD CHAINING−an obvious alternative to backward chaining is forward chaining of the actions/responses making up a chain, as depicted earlier.

• FACILITATING SKILLS/KNOWLEDGE−if certain skills/ knowledge have general application to what is being learned, then they can be taught first.

• GROUPED OBJECTIVES−where the skills/knowledge to be learned are closely related (e.g., share common stimuli, etc.), then it may prove desirable to group these and teach them simultaneously. This is illustrated in the Classifying Quadrilaterals frame sequence (Appendix B), where four similar concepts are taught simultaneously rather than separately in different frame sequences.

• "SHAPING SEQUENCES−where there is a chain of actions or responses to be learned, such as the performance problem-solving steps discussed under backward chaining above, a shaping sequence can be used. Each frame sequence teaches the entire chain, starting with simple versions and moving toward increasingly complex ones until the end-of-program objective has been realized. This is comparable to the shaping *strategy* described above.

Summary of Operational Description of PI

In this section I have discussed the following operational aspects of PI programs:

• The functional parts of PI frame sequences (exercises, lessons) as defined in Table 2 and illustrated by two samples,

Calculating Batting Averages (Appendix A) and Classifying Quadrilaterals (Appendix B).
- Analysis of testing stimuli or items; specifically:
  - The basic item forms, constructed-response (for recall) and multiple-choice (for recognition).
  - The general structure of items—input stimuli, response mechanisms, and feedback—and specifics of these.
  - The content of items in relation to their intended functions—criterion, sub-criterion, and prerequisite items as these relate to task analysis of the desired on-the-job performances for which the PI is supposed to prepare the learner.
  - Other/special items to strengthen covert (mental) response elements of the criterion behavior or skills/ knowledge being taught in a frame sequence.
- Analysis of teaching stimuli; specifically:
  - Various forms of teaching stimuli.
  - Design of the content and functions of teaching stimuli in relation to the nature of the criterion behavior or skills/knowledge being taught (e.g., algorithms-models for chains, definitions-examples for discriminations/ generalizations).
- PI strategies; specifically:
  - Basic, general strategies (e.g., Table 2).
  - Specific strategies for combining teaching and testing stimuli for the initial and intermediate (priming and prompting) parts of frame sequences.
- Sequencing of PI end-of-program objectives and sub-objectives.

References
(OPERATIONAL USE section)

Alden, J. *Backward Chaining* (Instructional Design Library). Englewood Cliffs, N.J.: Educational Technology Publications, 1978.

Gilbert, T.F. Mathetics: II. The Design of Teaching Exercises. *Journal of Mathetics*, 1962, Vol. 2.

Harless, J.H. *Ounce of Analysis*. McLean, Va.: Harless Performance Guild, Inc., 1975.

IV.

DESIGN FORMAT

We have already examined the functional parts of a programmed frame sequence (exercise, lesson) and their organization; and we have analyzed two samples. My aim in this section is to extend the discussion of the organization of PI frame sequences to the overall design format, organization, or structure of a PI program composed of a number of the kinds of frame sequences you've already examined.

An outline or table of contents for a hypothetical PI text is shown in Table 5.

The inclusion of separate illustrative/reference materials in a PI package is done typically for either of two reasons:

- The illustrative/reference material must be referred to frequently, which makes it inconvenient if printed within the PI text (or expensive if repeated in it).

- The illustrative/reference material is not practical to include within the PI text (e.g., color photographs which if printed in the PI text boost its cost greatly, nonprint media, materials simply too big to fit the page size, etc.).

Techniques that have been used for illustrative/reference materials that require frequent reference include foldouts bound at the back of a PI text or perforated back pages that can be removed as needed.

Table 5

*Outline/Table of Contents
for Hypothetical PI Text*

NOTE: The material below assumes two printed texts, the PI text and an accompanying separate reference booklet containing job aids and illustrative material. The PI text teaches the use of the job aids.

COVER
TITLE PAGE WITH COPYRIGHT/PROPRIETARY STATUS INFORMATION
TABLE OF CONTENTS
PREFACE AND ACKNOWLEDGMENTS
UNIT 1—INTRODUCTION (the what, why, and who for the total program)
UNIT 2—CRITERION PRETEST (for the total program; may be separate)
UNIT 3—PREREQUISITES TEST (for the total program; may be separate)
UNIT 4—TOPIC A (Assume 2 objectives, A-1 and A-2)
- Introduction/preview (Objective A-1)
- Criterion pretest (to branch to Unit 4, Objective A-2)
- Prerequisite review/test (for Unit 4)*
- Teaching-testing section (Objective A-1)
  −Initial teaching (demonstrate, prime)
  −Intermediate teaching (prompt)
  −Testing (release, perform)
- Practice-isolated (Objective A-1)
- Review/summary (Objective A-1)
- Introduction/preview (Objective A-2)
  (criterion pretest, prerequisites, teaching-testing)
- Practice-isolated (Objective A-2)
- Review/summary (Objectives A-1, A-2)
- Practice-integrated (Objectives A-1, A-2)

*These prerequisite tests should not block further progress, but branch into remedial instruction. If the learner lacks all or many of the prerequisites for the overall program, this should be determined via the Unit 3 test.

Table 5 (Continued)

UNIT 5–TOPIC B (Assume 1 objective, B-1)
- Introduction/preview (Objective B-1)
- Criterion pretest (branch to Interim Test) (prerequisites, teaching-testing)
- Practice-isolated (Objective B-1)
- Review/summary (Objectives A-1, A-2, B-1)

INTERIM TEST (Practice-integrated, Objectives A-1, A-2, B-1)

UNIT 6–TOPIC C

NOTE: This and additional units as needed for the "topics," with each unit structured like those above depending on the number of objectives and with further interim tests as appropriate based on the complexity and number of "topics."

UNIT N–CRITERION POSTTEST (for total program; may be separate)

BIBLIOGRAPHY/REFERENCES/RESOURCES

INDEX/GLOSSARY

Additional design format decisions associated with PI programs are the following:

- *Page layout*—frames can go down the page as in the usual text or they can be laid out in various other arrangements. Straightforward down-the-page layouts are preferable, in my ·judgment, as they generally avoid complex production problems that can arise with other layouts.

- *Feedback*—the location of the feedback for frames does present a problem, since research shows clearly that where the feedback is readily visible (such as just below its frame), there is a strong tendency to "peek" at it before responding, and that preventing "peeking" facilitates learning. Nonetheless, for practical reasons, it is preferable to have it located just below its frame with some clear separation, such as a line.

  —one important "rule" about feedback is that it conform in its layout to the layout of the response portion of the frame to facilitate convenient comparing of learner responses with the feedback.

  —including explanatory information in the feedback— commentary feedback—can have two potential advantages: it can serve to reduce the ease of inadvertent peeking and where certain learner errors are particularly important, commentary feedback can be used to explain the why and why not of correct and incorrect answers or responses.

- *Response mechanisms* deserve careful planning:

  —for *constructed-response* items, it is important to provide sufficient space for the written responses.

  —for *multiple-choice* items, it is important to make clear from the start if there will be items on occasion that will have more than one correct choice, since our prior experience with multiple-choice is just one correct choice (which is needlessly limiting on really good multiple-choice items).

- *Directions*—it is almost always desirable, if not necessary, to provide directions for how best to use a PI program, such as first responding to the items and then checking the feedback, actually writing the responses to all items, etc. These can be put as a kind of "preface" at the start, but I recommend they be incorporated into the initial frames to minimize the risk of their not being read (or being forgotten).

- *Progress plotters*—are worth considering for PI programs of substantial size having a number of frame sequences (exercises, lessons). Progress plotters show the sequence and indicate the learner's present position in the sequence. For example, a progress plotter for this book might appear at the start of each section and look something like this:

INTRODUCTION
USE
OPERATIONAL DESCRIPTION
DESIGN FORMAT ←   You are here
OUTCOMES
DEVELOPMENT GUIDE
CONCLUDING COMMENTS

In conclusion, effective communication and teaching with PI programs such as programmed texts requires careful attention to such things as captions and headings, placing boxes around key information, using tables and the like to highlight comparisons in teaching information/stimuli, the use of special typefaces, indenting, underlining, etc., to highlight key terms and information, and so on—in effect, all of the things that can contribute to making *any* book more readable and understandable.

V.

OUTCOMES

Let's assume that the need for PI meets the conditions stated in the section on USE of PI. What benefits can you reasonably expect from PI? And what benefits can you reasonably expect for your learners?

In my experience, there are two potential benefits that are the most significant and which seem to me to apply equally well to both the learners and to the instructional programmers responsible for the PI:

- Empirical tryouts and validation
- Frequent responding with immediate feedback.

Empirical Tryouts and Validation

You can develop a PI program *without* conducting any tryouts or a formal test of its validity as a means of instruction. Simply write it and then sell or use it. Unfortunately, this appears true of the great bulk of the PI texts that have been published commercially. Fortunately, this appears to be increasingly less true of PI developed for internal training purposes. The reasons for this difference are, I think, as follows:

- Buyers of commercially-published PI texts are not yet aware enough as consumers that the instructional effectiveness of PI can in fact be assured through empirical tryouts and valida-

53

tion. PI texts are bought on the basis of their subject matters rather than claims of guaranteed learning outcomes. Thus, there is no real advantage to publishers—only additional costs—to require that PI texts be tested before being published.*

- Developers of PI for internal training in business/industry and similar situations are much more likely to be concerned about learning outcomes, since this is often the basis for justifying the investment in PI. Thus, the potential benefits from testing are clearly perceived and understood and the cost of such testing much more likely to be part of PI development budgets.

Just what are these alleged benefits from developmental tryouts and empirical validation of PI programs? And what do these terms mean, anyway?

Table 6 defines and states the intended benefits from two kinds of testing of PI programs: developmental tryouts and validation.

Frequent Responding with
Immediate Feedback

An especially powerful feature of PI programs is their reliance on *active* responding (versus passive reading). This is achieved through the use of items and their accompanying feedback. Unlike more "passive" forms of instruction (e.g., the lecture or audiovisual show), the learner cannot simply "tune out" the instructional inputs. If the learner does stop responding, the PI "sits and waits" (so to speak) for the learner to resume. This feature of frequent responding with immediate feedback enables PI to offer these benefits:

---

*There are exceptions. For example, the library of PI texts published by John Wiley under the direction of Judith Vantrease Wilson are subject to testing prior to publication.

Table 6

*Definition and Intended Benefits
of Testing of PI*

TYPE OF TESTING	DEFINITION	INTENDED BENEFITS
DEVELOPMENTAL TRYOUTS	Program administered to one person (or a small group) under informal conditions. Learners ask to write all responses and to add comments wherever they find sources of confusion, unnecessary repetition, etc. Programmer may interact with learner during the tryouts and always goes over the program frame-by-frame afterwards. Formal criterion posttest may or may not be used.	Basically, to "de-bug" the program by having learners' incorrect responses and comments reveal trouble spots, such as: • Confusing teaching information/stimuli or testing items • Unnecessarily repetitive material or unnecessary material • Points where additional teaching/testing seems needed • Sequence and strategy problems and so on.
VALIDATION TESTS	Program administered to a group of learners representative of the target audience under controlled conditions	Basically, to make sure that the program is sufficiently effective to justify its field implementation.

Table 6 (Continued)

TYPE OF TESTING	DEFINITION	INTENDED BENEFITS
VALIDATION TESTS	designed to match the later field use conditions.

Formal criterion posttest.

Learner feedback data via anonymous form.

Within-program and posttest errors and learner feedback used to evaluate both program validity and its acceptance by learners. | If the program fails to meet the validation criterion (e.g., 90% of learners score 90% or better on posttest), the program may require further revision and re-validation prior to field implementation. |

- Almost continuously throughout the instruction the learner can demonstrate overtly the skills/knowledge being learned.

- At the same time, the learner can detect immediately any "mislearning" that is occurring from the immediate feedback and take suitable corrective actions.

A very substantial body of experimental research exists to support the claim that these two benefits act to promote effective, efficient learning.

There is a special benefit to the instructional programmer from this feature of frequent responding in PI programs. The overt responses of the learners provide a unique record of the impact of the instruction, frame-by-frame. Thus, the programmer can detect fairly precisely flaws in material and— aided by comments from the learners—take steps to improve the program by revising it to correct for these flaws.

In effect, the frequent responding feature of PI makes possible the kind of developmental tryouts described in Table 6.

The "Boredom" Question

The frequent responding required by PI programs can result in "boredom"—learners complaining about how boring it is. Historically, this has been a chronic problem.

Boredom complaints can be understood, in part, by comparing PI as an active instructional method with the more passive kinds to which learners are likely accustomed. PI demands—for the learner to learn what it teaches—that the learner do the "work" necessary for the learning to occur. The learner must, to achieve the maximum benefit, process each "frame" carefully: examine it, think about it, respond to it, and then compare the responses with the feedback. This requires an expenditure of effort and time (i.e., work) that makes it understandable that under certain conditions the learner may well become "bored":

- What the PI teaches is not perceived as really relevant to the learner's needs—result, as with any form of instruction, can be insufficient motivation and boredom.

- The behaviors (skills/knowledge) being learned are not perceived as simulating closely enough the things the learner is expected or required to do on the job upon completing the instruction—result, as with any form of instruction, can be insufficient motivation and boredom.

- The "step-size" is too small, meaning that the frame sequences and frames within them produce such small learning gains that the learner has difficulty perceiving that any real progress is occurring, or that the level of instruction is somewhat insulting. The result, perhaps peculiar primarily to PI due to its requirement for frequent overt responding, can be insufficient motivation and boredom.

When the boredom-including conditions described above are absent from PI programs, experience shows that boredom is unlikely to be a learner complaint. Keep in mind, however, that *imposed* instruction is rarely "fun." So-called "learning for the sake of learning" is found primarily when the learners are learning what they have decided is worth learning at the time they feel like doing the work required to learn it!

Automatic/Guaranteed Learning

Probably the single most important overall benefit of PI is the fact that when properly developed and empirically validated it can produce the desired learning automatically in a guaranteed manner.

- PI learning can be said to be AUTOMATIC in the sense that if the learner goes through the program in the prescribed manner—responding to each item along the way and checking the feedback—learning will necessarily result. For this reason, the learner does not have to apply special studying skills.

- PI learning can be said to be GUARANTEED to the extent

that the program has been empirically validated—formal testing has shown that it does in fact produce the desired learning in learners representative of the target audience for which it is intended.

In Summary

In deciding whether to use PI, you should always consider whether the following key advantages and benefits are sufficiently worthwhile to you and your learners to justify the necessary investment in developing PI:

ADVANTAGES	BENEFITS
Programmed, frequent responding, with immediate feedback.	Automatic learning via self-instruction.
Empirically-validated PI program.	Guaranteed learning of the desired skills/knowledge.

VI.

DEVELOPMENTAL GUIDE
A PROGRAMMED INSTRUCTION
DEVELOPMENT MODEL

Generally speaking, it is common practice among instructional technologists to develop programmed instruction products via a systematic process. Thus, the term INSTRUCTIONAL DEVELOPMENT PROCESS is sometimes used. As noted in the introduction to this book, some use the term programmed instruction to identify this process, even if the resulting instruction is, strictly speaking, not PI as defined in this book.

The PI development process differs, of course, depending on who is carrying it out, for what purposes, and the nature of the PI being developed. For example, where an individual programmer who is also a subject matter specialist develops a PI program, the process may well differ substantially from that used when a team of people is involved. For this reason, you may encounter references to instructional development MODELS. By model is meant the particular process used by a particular individual or group.

What I will describe in this section is one particular model for PI development. In writing this model, I have tried to ensure the following:

- The model will be an *idealized* model that incorporates the major or primary characteristics of various specific models with which I am familiar.*

- The model is stated in the form of a sequence of steps that I believe are basic to a PI development model (even though it is most certainly neither assumed nor required that one always performs all of the steps or necessarily performs them in the order listed).

- The model will be of practical use to you as a *general* guide to the development of PI programs. At the same time, I must WARN you that you can apply the model only if you have the necessary skills/knowledge. By itself, the model is not sufficient to guide your development of PI programs.

Steps in an Idealized PI Development Model**

Step 1   TRAINING NEEDS ASSESSMENT

- *Performance deficiencies*—identify actual/anticipated performance deficiencies or problems requiring some form of remedy or solution.

- *Skill/knowledge deficits*—identify those performance deficiencies involving skill/knowledge deficits for which some form of instruction/job aids are appropriate remedies or solutions.

*Three models have exerted the major influence on my thinking: the AT&T *Training Development Standards* (1973); Harless' "Analysis and Instructional Design Workshop" (1976); and *Systematic Course Design for the Health Fields* by Segall, Vanderschmidt, Burglass, and Frostman (1975). All three of these instructional development models reflect the pioneering formulations by Gilbert, referenced earlier.

**The first *three* steps described are typically done concurrently in connection with an overall effort to ensure cost-effective, job-relevant instruction/job aids.

- *Worth*—determine or estimate whether the cost of developing the instruction/job aids is justified by the anticipated dollars or other benefits from their effective use.

Step 2   TASK ANALYSIS

- *Mastery specification*—analyze and specify the on-the-job (or other) tasks involved to establish the desired or mastery performance as the basis for:

  —designing the content and format of job aids (see Step 6)

  —deriving end-of-program objectives (see Step 4)

Step 3   TARGET AUDIENCE ANALYSIS

- *Target audience characteristics*—identify their entry skills/ knowledge and other characteristics sufficiently to permit informed decisions about:

  —prerequisites and the need to provide within-program branching (based on criterion pretests, prerequisite tests), formal remedial instruction, and minimum entry requirements for the PI

  —media requirements associated with special characteristics (e.g., audio inputs where reading skills are a problem, etc.)

  —selection of representative learners for developmental tryouts and validation testing.

Step 4   END-OF-PROGRAM OBJECTIVES
          AND CRITERION TESTS

- *Objectives*—derive from the preceding analyses the end-of-program (terminal) objectives, taking into account:

—adequate *behavioral* specification (i.e., "behavioral objectives" that make clear the input stimuli, response mechanisms, feedback criteria)

—analysis of critical *learning problems* (e.g., discriminations and generalizations, response chains or sequences, psychomotor proficiencies, rote associations), which affect media/simulation decisions

—desired *level-of-learning*, including

- the optimum degree of approximation or simulation of on-the-job tasks that is feasible in terms of cost and other practical considerations (media/simulation decisions)

- recall requirements (short- and long-term), which affect decisions about isolated/integrated practice.

NOTE: End-of-program objectives can specify either guidance with job aids or recall from instruction or combinations of these. Sub-objectives within end-of-program objectives and enabling objectives are usually specified later (see Step 5).

- *Criterion tests*—specify the criterion tests needed to measure the attainment of the end-of-program objectives.

NOTE: The actual development of the criterion test items often occurs later in the process, partly because the objectives may be revised during the instructional design activities (Step 5).

Step 5 INSTRUCTIONAL DESIGN
(For Job Aids Design, See Step 6)

- *Overall design*—establish the general, overall design of the program, including such aspects as:

  —*media* (print/nonprint components appropriate to the objectives, target audience characteristics, and resources available)

  —*methods* (application/practice exercises appropriate to the objectives—hands-on demonstrations, in-basket and other case problems, role-playing, etc.)

  —*pretesting*, including

  - criterion pretest for the program itself and for by-passing or skipping units within the program

  - prerequisite tests for either preventing unqualified learners from taking the instruction or providing within-program branching into remedial instruction

  —*sequence* (the "main path" in which the objectives will be taught and options for variations—"topical" outline or table of contents or what some call a course "map" or "profile")

  —*supplemental materials* (separate illustrative/reference materials, which may include job aids the PI will teach the learners how to use)

  —*"teacher" involvement* (intended role of an instructor, which may require a separate administration manual)

—time requirements (maximum/minimum time constraints, if any; handling of individual differences in
learning times; etc.)

and other design decisions that may be feasible at this
stage but are often made later in PI development (Steps
7-8):

—format/layout (distribution of frames on pages, response
mechanisms, feedback location and types, etc.)

—physical package (the estimated scope of the PI package,
such as total number of pages, media requirements, etc.)

—special features (within-program directions for the
learner, progress plotter, supplemental activities, glossary, index, etc.)

- *General strategies*—decide the general organization or
  structure of the frame sequences (exercises, lessons), such
  as that described in Table 2.

- *Specific strategies*—determine as feasible at this stage how
  each objective (or set of related objectives to be taught
  concurrently) will be taught; that is, specific strategies as
  described in the section on Operational Description of this
  book.

  NOTE: Decisions regarding specific strategies may often be
  made in connection with the actual development of
  specific frame sequences; see Step 7.

Step 6   JOB AIDS DESIGN

NOTE: The analyses in Steps 1-3 normally result in

decisions as to those tasks for which on-the-job guidance with job aids is preferable to recall from instruction. Here we are concerned with the specifics of job aids design, their content and format. Since it is typical that developing job aids for OTJ guidance involves concurrent development of PI for teaching how to use the job aids, job aids may be among the supplemental materials identified in the overall design (Step 5). It is especially important in such cases that job aids design should precede PI instructional design, to ensure that the latter reflects the job aids in question; i.e., Step 6 before Step 5.

- *Content of job aids*—specify the content (e.g, within-task steps) to be covered by a given job aid. This may have been done during the Step 2, task analysis, which can be formatted as at least a first approximation of the job aid(s) desired. In other words, the content of the typical job aid derives directly from the task analysis of the desired or mastery OTJ performance to be guided by the job aid.

- *Format of job aids*—decide the particular format for each job aid based on the nature of the task to be guided and the associated skills/knowledge (e.g., checklist, decision table, flowchart, list of directions or guidelines, worksheet, etc.).

Step 7 INSTRUCTION/JOB AIDS DEVELOPMENT (Based on Steps 5-6)

- *Construct the specific job aids required*—produce prototypes for developmental tryouts.

- *Write the criterion test items* for the job aids, based on the criterion test specifications from Step 4.

• *Write the frame sequences (exercises, lessons)* for each objective or sub-objective, including job aid objectives— that is, produce the materials called for by the instructional design (Step 5), usually as follows:

—*Decide the specific strategy*, if not decided previously (e.g., algorithmic, definitional, etc.) for a given frame sequence

—*criterion items* as needed for the teaching-testing and isolated/integrated practice sections of a given frame sequence

—*initial teaching frames*—the teaching and testing stimuli for a given frame sequence (the demonstrate/prime function)

—*intermediate teaching frames*—the teaching and testing stimuli for the prompting function, as needed (including other/special items) for a given frame sequence

—*pretest frames* (criterion pretest and prerequisite test frames as called for by the design)

—*previews, reviews/summaries* for a given frame sequence.

NOTE: The experienced instructional programmer will, of course, develop an individual "style" for developing the components above. Quite typically, for example, the PI material will be written in its normal instructional "flow"—the preview, pretesting (criterion, prerequisites), initial teaching, intermediate teaching, testing, practice (isolated, integrated), review/summary in that order for each frame sequence in the order it will occur in the total PI program.

- *Write the supplemental materials*—glossary, index, progress plotter, table of contents, etc. (see the Design Format section).

Step 8 PRODUCE PROTOTYPES FOR TESTING

NOTE: Based on the preceding steps, it is now feasible to produce prototypes (drafts) of the instruction/job aids for developmental tryouts. While the details of prototype production are beyond the scope of this development guide, it is important in my experience to ensure the following:

- *Editing-PI*—have an experienced instructional programmer "edit" the material prior to testing. This can be invaluable for identifying likely problems that may warrant revisions of the instruction/job aids prior to testing.

- *Editing-technical*—it is equally important to have the material reviewed by a qualified subject matter expert/ specialist to ensure that the content is technically accurate prior to testing.

- *Editing-learner*—certain kinds of "errors" in the material (e.g., incorrect feedback) can often only be spotted by an individual who goes through the material as a "learner." Thus, to minimize feedback and other typographical errors likely to interfere with learning, it is best to have at least one person go through the material as a "learner" prior to testing. This can be the same person who serves as the PI-editor.

Step 9 DEVELOPMENTAL TRYOUTS

NOTE: Given the prototype materials from Step 8, you

can conduct developmental tryouts to "de-bug" the PI and job aids. Since the purpose is to identify and correct problems in the material, it may not be essential to have a formal criterion posttest, although it is preferable. Among the key considerations in developmental tryouts are the following:

- *Attitudes*—in explaining the developmental tryout to the learners, emphasis should be placed on the purpose; that is, to test the material rather than to test the learner, to identify problems in the material so that revisions can be made to improve it.

- *Learners*—initial developmental tryout learners should, in my judgment, be "better" rather than "poorer" learners, since problems they encounter will most likely also be problems for others. Subsequent tryouts can then use "average" and "poorer" learners (whatever that means).

- *Method*—developmental tryouts work best with one or a small group of learners and key things to include are:

  —crossing out rather than erasing when changing responses to items (use ball-point pens)

  —encourage writing of comments right in the materials (circling or underlining problem words, phrases, etc.)

  —asking questions as they arise (but avoid "lecturing" in response, which just contaminates the results)

  —conducting a frame-by-frame review of the material afterwards with every encouragement to identify specific problems and to suggest revisions.

- *Results*—developmental tryouts are not intended to "prove" that the material works; they are successful to the extent that they reveal specific problems in the material (e.g., things to delete, expand, leave as is, or modify).

NOTE: When you conduct developmental tryouts of *your* materials, be especially wary of the learners' natural social tendency to avoid being critical. As feasible, have someone else conduct the tryouts.

Step 10   VALIDATION TESTING

NOTE: When the results from developmental tryouts indicate that the PI (including job aids) works sufficiently well to justify investment in a more controlled, formal testing, validation testing should be conducted under conditions that resemble as closely as practicable the actual field conditions. Among the key considerations are these:

- *Acceptance*—some type of learner feedback form should be administered at the end of the test to determine the learners' reactions to the material and should be anonymous. For long programs, it may be desirable to obtain such learner feedback at appropriate points within the program. Specifics of learner feedback forms are beyond the scope of this book.

- *Attitudes*—in explaining the validation test to the learners (as well as in arranging for their participation), it is important that they be "motivated" to do their best and that they understand fully the nature and purpose of the validation testing.

- *Learners*—deciding the number of learners to include and their characteristics is a perennial problem in PI validation tests. They must, of course, be genuinely representative of the target audience, since otherwise the validation results will have questionable validity. My personal bias is to have at least 10 participants *selected by the "client"* (the ultimate user who's paying the "bill"). As feasible, I prefer that at least half of them represent those judged (on whatever basis available) as "below average" to ensure that the program works satisfactorily for those learners most likely to experience difficulties.

- *Method*—should match as closely as feasible the later field conditions:

  —*orientation*

  —*criterion pretest* (optional)

  —*prerequisites test* (optional)

  —*program administration*

  —*criterion posttest*

  —*participant reactions* (feedback form, open discussion)

- *Results*—performance on the criterion posttest is, of course, the critical data. In using posttest performance data to decide whether the PI is valid enough to warrant its field use, key things to keep in mind are:

  —*validation criteria* (ideally, there should be stated criteria for deciding if the PI is valid, such as 90% of the learners scoring 90% or higher on the posttest; this is a complicated problem, however, and beyond the scope of this book.

—further revisions (even when the program achieves 90/90 results, there will always be some problems revealed that require further revisions, based on data of the kind discussed under Step 9; whether such revisions require another validation test is basically a matter of judgment).

Step 11 FIELD IMPLEMENTATION AND
FOLLOW-UP EVALUATION

NOTE: When the PI has been validated, its production for and field implementation follows. These aspects warrant consideration.

• *Administration manual*—where the PI is administered by an instructor, an administration manual may be needed (i.e., where various instructors will be responsible). Ideally, this should be developed and evaluated in connection with the validation testing by having the instructors conduct the validation testing using the manual. The development of administration manuals is beyond the scope of this book.

• *Field modifications*—as desirable/feasible, some mechanism should be established for further data collection during at least the initial phases of field implementation for purposes of further improvement of the materials, as well as for updating content when necessary.

• *Follow-up evaluation*—while validation is obviously crucial, a valid program is justified ultimately by virtue of its enabling the learners to acquire skills/knowledge that *transfer* to and are used on the job. Determining the extent of such transfer requires follow-up evaluation; for discussion of this problem, see Smith and Corbett (1976).

Comments

What follows are comments about selected aspects of the development guide.

Step 2, TASK ANALYSIS. Basically task analysis means analyzing and specifying behavior or performance. As such, it occurs throughout the process. I have used it to label Step 2 because historically the term has been used primarily to identify the analysis and specification of on-the-job performance, especially OTJ mastery.

Step 4, END-OF-PROGRAM OBJECTIVES AND CRITERION TESTS. A fairly recent concept is that of validating the criterion test by administering it to both master performers and "neophytes" to make sure that it does in fact measure validly the desired or mastery performance and associated skills/knowledge.

Step 5, INSTRUCTIONAL DESIGN. While ideally media/ simulation decisions should be based on analysis of learning problems, budgeting requirements often require that these decisions be made quite early in the process, even before formal specification of objectives.

Step 6, JOB AIDS DESIGN. Too many instructional programmers fail, I believe, to realize how job aids development is part-and-parcel of the development of PI and other forms of instruction. My bias is this: always think first and foremost of the possibility of using job aids to remedy skill/knowledge deficits (actual or anticipated) and use PI (or other instruction) only if the nature of the tasks rules out job aids. In other words, job aids decisions, design, development, implementation, and evaluation are to me an integral part of the responsibilities of instructional programmers.

Step 9, DEVELOPMENTAL TRYOUTS. Many professional practitioners would agree with me that this is the "heart" of successful PI development. There is nothing quite so enlightening—often painfully enlightening—as actually having learners try to learn from your material!

Step 10, VALIDATION TESTING. Fundamental to the concept of PI is the validation of programs prior to field use.

- *Pretests* (criterion/prerequisites)—while it is appealing in theory to include criterion and prerequisites pretests for the program, they do present some serious problems:

  —*criterion pretests* can be boring and potentially onerous to the extent that they require the learner to invest substantial effort and time merely demonstrating that he/she cannot do already what the PI teaches; avoid criterion pretesting if there are reasonable grounds for assuming that all or most of the learners will enter the PI lacking the skills/knowledge taught by it; deal with individual differences via within-program branching as appropriate/feasible.

  —*prerequisite tests* pose an especially difficult problem, as they imply that a learner can be "washed-out" as not ready for the PI, and providing formal remedial instruction can be quite costly; the optimum solution is to minimize the need for prerequisite testing—for example, by having the means for selecting the target audience ensure that all or most of them will have adequate prerequisite skill/knowledge.

- *Criterion posttests*—while these are obviously essential in validation testing to determine how well the PI works, once the PI program has been proven adequately valid, use of criterion posttests in field implementation should be based on different considerations which may permit it to be shortened:

—checking that there is no deterioration in the impact of the material in field use

—providing means for identifying specific weakness of learners as a basis for individualized remedial assistance

—"certification" of learners when appropriate or required.

In conclusion, let me emphasize strongly that the steps listed in this idealized PI development model are general guidelines, not a "straight-jacket"! In actual practice, you'll find a wide diversity of applications of such models. The crucial thing is that when you are involved in developing PI, you give adequate attention to the concerns stated in the various steps I have described.

References
(DEVELOPMENTAL GUIDE section)

AT&T Training Development Standards. New York: AT&T, 1973. *Analysis and Instructional Design Workshop*, McLean, Va.: Harless Performance Guild, Inc., 1976.

Harless, J.H. *Analysis and Instructional Design Workshop*. McLean, Va.: Harless Performance Guild, Inc., 1976.

Segall, A., H. Vanderschmidt, R. Burglass and T. Frostman. *Systematic Course Design for the Health Fields*. New York: John Wiley, 1975.

Smith, M. and A. Corbett. Exchanging Ideas on Evaluation: 1. Basic Questions. *NSPI Journal*, July 1976, *15*(8).

VII.

RESOURCES

Here are some of the resource materials that may be of help to you in expanding your skills/knowledge in PI.

☐ Holland, Solomon, Doran, and Frezza's *The Analysis of Behavior in Planning Instruction*, Reading, Ma.: Addison-Wesley, 1976. An excellent compendium of articles supported by commentary.

☐ Harless' *Ounce of Analysis* and Harless and Lineberry's *Turning Kids On and Off*, McLean, Va.: Harless Performance Guild, Inc., 1973. Two first-rate examples of present-day PI concepts and techniques.

☐ Segall, Vanderschmidt, Burglass, and Frostman's *Systematic Course Design for the Health Fields*, New York: John Wiley, 1975. An excellent exposition of a model for systematic design of instruction.

☐ Susan Markle's *Good Frames and Bad*, New York: John Wiley, 1969 (2nd ed.). One of the few empirically tested PI texts available that teaches many key aspects of PI.

☐ Robert Mager's *Measuring Instructional Intent*, Belmont, Ca.: Lear Siegler, Inc./Fearon Publishers, 1973. Very helpful in ensuring that your criterion items match the associated instructional objectives.

VIII.

CONCLUDING COMMENTS

In the early developmental days of PI, certain "issues" tended to be paramount—arguments about so-called "linear" and "branching" techniques, arguments about "step size" (early PI tended to emphasize "small" frames with but one or two responses per frame), and so on.

As PI has matured to its present status, these issues have become of historical interest only. These days PI programmers are concerned with such things as:

- Using a PI development model or process that ensures that PI will be a cost-effective, job-relevant means for helping learners to acquire needed skills/knowledge—and *not* using PI when job aids or other less expensive forms on instruction are better ways to remedy the performance problems in question.

- Using whatever frame and item types, media, and packaging techniques that appear likely to ensure effective learning.

- Incorporating PI into instructional or training programs or systems that emphasize effective implementation and follow-up evaluation of the transfer of what the PI teaches to the actual job situation.

- Teaching only those criterion behaviors or skills/knowledge for which less tightly-programmed instruction (such as "individualized instruction" with learning activity packages") appear insufficient to guarantee adequate learning.

Generally, PI in business/industry and similar situations is used under the guidance of an instructor or instructional manager responsible for distributing the material, answering questions, giving feedback on criterion tests, conducting question-and-answer discussions after lessons, and so on.

PI is very much alive today. Whatever the form of its delivery—audiovisual show, computer, programmed text, etc.—it offers a powerful "tool" for achieving empirically-validated ("guaranteed") learning. But its cost-effective use depends critically on careful analysis of the "need" and systematic development of the PI designed to meet that need.

Stated another way, as a *product* PI can offer tremendous benefits, but only to the extent that the PI product is developed via a systematic *process*.

IX.

APPENDIX A

SAMPLE FRAME SEQUENCE:
CALCULATING BATTING AVERAGES

This hypothetical PI program is used to illustrate the basic structure of a frame-sequence (exercise, lesson) in programmed text format. It has not been tested and the language is probably more complex then that suitable for the alleged target audience of Little League baseball players. The feedback for frames has been omitted to save space.

....

COVER   CALCULATING BATTING AVERAGES

A Teach-Yourself Book for Little Leaguers

Before using this book, be sure you have completed these books:

- Keeping Score! How to Use a Scorecard
- Counting Official Times at Bat
- Doing Long Division with Decimal Points

Copyright © 1978 Donald H. Bullock

....

FRAME 1   WHAT'S THIS BOOK ALL ABOUT?

As a Little Leaguer, you'll want to keep track of your hitting.

As you know, major league ballplayers keep track of their hitting with something called the BATTING AVERAGE.

This book lets you teach yourself how to calculate YOUR batting average to keep track of how well you're hitting.

TURN TO THE NEXT PAGE AND LET'S GET STARTED!

···

FRAME 2   A TEST ON CALCULATING BATTING AVERAGES

Perhaps you already know how to calculate batting averages.

If so, do the batting average problems below and then ask your coach or someone else to score your answers.

If you don't already know how to calculate batting averages, GO ON TO THE NEXT PAGE.

1. In one game a player hit a single, a double, walked once, struckout once, and was safe on an error.

   What was his hitting average? .... (WRITE THE ANSWER)

2. In one season a player had this batting record:

4 walks	7 groundouts	2 sacrifices
5 singles	5 flyouts	3 times safe on
2 doubles	3 foulouts	errors
1 homerun	6 strikeouts	

   What was his batting average? .... (WRITE THE ANSWER)

3. Up to the last game of the season, a player's batting average was .250 (20 times at bat, 5 hits). In the final game, he batted five-for-five.

What was his batting average for the season? ....

....

FRAME 3   SOME THINGS YOU HAVE TO KNOW BEFORE USING THIS BOOK

Your batting average is based on OFFICIAL TIMES AT BAT. You should know how to count these from the book, "Counting Official Times at Bat."

Just to make sure that you can count official times at bat (AB), DRAW A LINE UNDER each thing below that counts as a time at bat.

single	groundout	sacrifice
dobule	flyout	safe on error
triple	foulout	safe on fielder's
homerun	strikeout	choice

Ask your coach or someone else to score this for you.

....

FRAME 4   SOMETHING ELSE YOU HAVE TO KNOW BEFORE USING THIS BOOK

To calculate batting averages, you have to already be able to do long division and put the decimal point in the right place. You should know this from school or from the book, "Doing Long Division with Decimal Points."

Just to make sure that you can do long divisions and put the decimal point where it belongs, do all of the problems below.

1. Divide 30 into 6. The answer is ....
BE SURE YOU PUT THE DECIMAL POINT WHERE IT BELONGS!

2. Divide 48 into 12. The answer is ....
HOW ABOUT THAT DECIMAL POINT?

3. Divide 39 into 13. The answer is ....
REMEMBER THE DECIMAL POINT

Ask your coach or someone else to score this for you.

....

FRAME 5   THE IDEA OF A BATTING AVERAGE

Your BATTING AVERAGE tells you the *percent* of times you get a hit for each time at bat.

For example, if you get a hit half of the times you're officially at bat, your batting average is .500 and we say you are batting "five hundred."

If you get three hits in ten times at bat, then you batted "three hundred." Your batting average is .300.

Let's learn how to calculate batting averages like .450 ("four-fifty"), or .200 ("two hundred").

GO ON TO THE NEXT PAGE

....

FRAME 6   HOW TO CALCULATE A BATTING AVERAGE

1. Count up the number of official times at bat.

2. Count up all the hits.

3. Divide the number of times at bat into the number of hits.

Like this: • BATTING AVERAGE

OFFICIAL TIMES AT BAT $\diagup$ HITS

For example: suppose you had 2 hits in 6 times at bat.

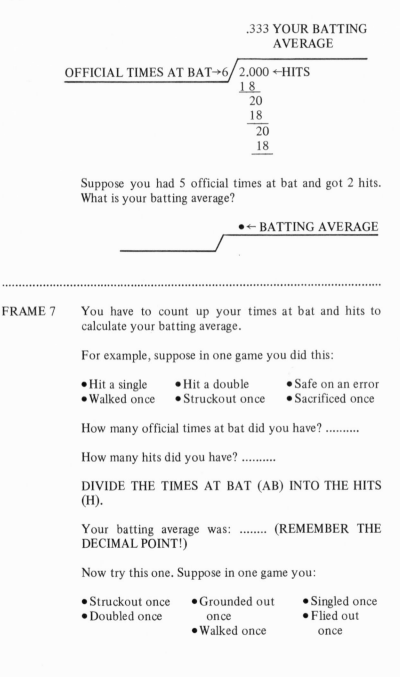

.333 YOUR BATTING
AVERAGE

OFFICIAL TIMES AT BAT→6/2.000 ←HITS
                        1 8
                        ‾20‾
                         18
                        ‾20‾
                         18
                        ‾‾‾

Suppose you had 5 official times at bat and got 2 hits.
What is your batting average?

•← BATTING AVERAGE

FRAME 7   You have to count up your times at bat and hits to
calculate your batting average.

For example, suppose in one game you did this:

• Hit a single   • Hit a double   • Safe on an error
• Walked once   • Struckout once   • Sacrificed once

How many official times at bat did you have? ....

How many hits did you have? ....

DIVIDE THE TIMES AT BAT (AB) INTO THE HITS
(H).

Your batting average was: .... (REMEMBER THE
DECIMAL POINT!)

Now try this one. Suppose in one game you:

• Struckout once   • Grounded out   • Singled once
• Doubled once   once   • Flied out
                    • Walked once   once

What's your batting average for that game? ....
(DECMIAL POINT?)

FRAME 8   Here's a player's record for five games:

- 3 singles   • 1 safe on error   • 4 hitouts
- 1 double   • 1 safe on fielder's   • 1 sacrifice
- 1 homerun   choice   • 1 strikeout

He had 12 official times at bat, 5 hits.

```
                .4166 ──→ round off to    .417 which is his
                                          batting average.
        12   5.0000
             4 8
             ───
              20
              12
             ───
              80
              72
             ───
              80
              72
             ───
               8  ← repeating remainder ──→
```

Suppose your record for the first games of the season
was:

- 5 singles   • 3 flyouts   • 2 safe on fielder's
- 2 doubles   • 2 foulouts   choice
- 1 homerun   • 3 strikeouts   • 1 sacrifice

Now what's your batting average for all of the games?

FRAME 10   [SERIES OF PROBLEMS AS IN FRAME 2, BUT WITH
               DATA PRESENTED IN THE FORM OF OFFICIAL
               SCORECARDS, WHICH THEY'VE ALREADY
               LEARNED TO INTERPRET.]

NOTE: This hypothetical program has been simplified to save space. Actually, Frame 9 should have a number of batting average calculation problems.

X.

APPENDIX B

SAMPLE FRAME SEQUENCE:
CLASSIFYING QUADRILATERALS

This hypothetical PI program is used to illustrate the basic structure of a frame-sequence (exercise, lesson) in programmed text format. It has not been tested and testing might well show that it attempts to teach too many concepts at once. Furthermore, I am not really qualified to vouch for the technical accuracy or soundness of the geometric concepts taught and suspect that qualified geometricists and geometry teachers might give me a very hard time in this respect!

....

FRAME 1   SOME SPECIAL FORMS OF QUADRILATERALS

In the previous lesson, you learned to classify certain forms of rectilinear quadrilaterals as parallelograms, rectangles, and squares—to classify certain 4-sided, straight-line geometric figures as:

- *Parallelograms*—rectilinear quadrilaterals with two pairs of parallel lines, right-angled or not.

- *Rectangles*—parallelograms that are right-angled and non-equilateral.

- *Squares*—parallelograms that are right-angled and equilateral.

89

You learned also that we normally call "parallelograms" those that are neither rectangles or squares, "rectangles" those that are not squares, and "squares" those that are not rectangles.

In this lesson you will learn to classify some special forms of rectilinear quadrilaterals: the RHOMBOID, the RHOMBUS, the TRAPEZIUM, and the TRAPEZOID.

Even though your curriculum objectives may not require your students to recognize these special forms, it is important for you to do so in order to answer their questions and to read the literature.

NO WRITTEN RESPONSE REQUIRED

....

FRAME 2   A TEST ON CLASSIFYING SPECIAL FORMS OF QUADRILATERALS

You may already know how to classify rectilinear quadrilaterals as rhomboids, rhombuses, trapeziums (trapezia), and trapezoids. If so, check yourself by taking the test below. If not, GO ON TO FRAME 3.

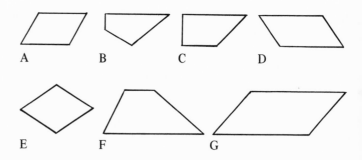

A   B   C   D

E   F   G

1. WRITE the letter for each RHOMBOID above: ....

2. WRITE the letter of each RHOMBUS above: ....

3. WRITE the letter of each TRAPEZIUM above: ....

4. WRITE the letter of each TRAPEZOID above: ....

—————————————————————————

FEEDBACK: 1. D, G; 2. A, E; 3. B; 4. C, F.

If you responded correctly to all four items above, SKIP-AHEAD TO FRAME 10.

....

FRAME 3   Certain discriminations are basic to this lesson. They are reviewed below.

A   B   C   D

1. WRITE the letter of each equilateral figure above: ....

2. WRITE the letter of each parallelogram above: ....

3. WRITE the letter of each rectilinear quadrilateral: ....

—————————————————————————

FEEDBACK: 1. A; 2. A, B, C (it's okay if you wrote only C on the basis that A is normally called a square and B a rectangle); 3. All four—A, B, C, D.

If you missed any of these, you may want to review the previous lesson.

....

FRAME 4   Certain expressions/terms are used in the teaching frames of this lesson. Thus, it is important that you know their meaning. They are reviewed below.

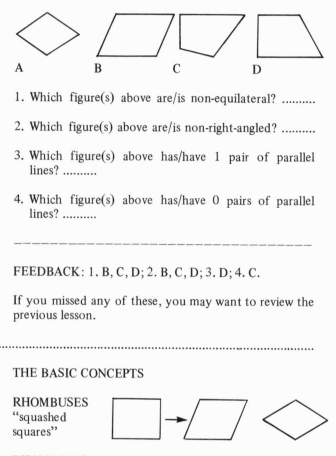

A   B   C   D

1. Which figure(s) above are/is non-equilateral? ....

2. Which figure(s) above are/is non-right-angled? ....

3. Which figure(s) above has/have 1 pair of parallel lines? ....

4. Which figure(s) above has/have 0 pairs of parallel lines? ....

FEEDBACK: 1. B, C, D; 2. B, C, D; 3. D; 4. C.

If you missed any of these, you may want to review the previous lesson.

....

FRAME 5   THE BASIC CONCEPTS

RHOMBUSES
"squashed
squares"

RHOMBOIDS
"wrecked
rectangles"

TRAPEZOIDS
"truncated
triangles"

TRAPEZIUMS
"zero pairza
parallels"

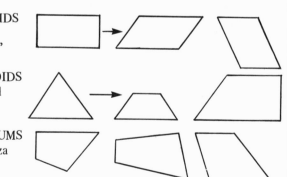

NO WRITTEN RESPONSE REQUIRED

....

FRAME 6   Four special forms of rectilinear quadrilaterals are
           defined and exemplified below.

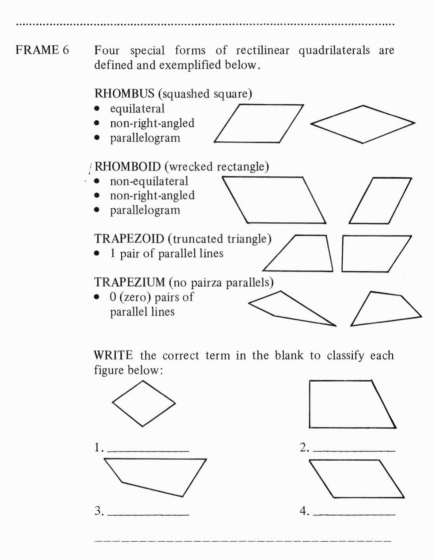

RHOMBUS (squashed square)
- equilateral
- non-right-angled
- parallelogram

RHOMBOID (wrecked rectangle)
- non-equilateral
- non-right-angled
- parallelogram

TRAPEZOID (truncated triangle)
- 1 pair of parallel lines

TRAPEZIUM (no pairza parallels)
- 0 (zero) pairs of
  parallel lines

WRITE the correct term in the blank to classify each
figure below:

1. _____   2. _____

3. _____   4. _____

— —

FEEDBACK: 1. rhombus; 2. trapezoid; 3. trapezium; 4.
rhomboid.

....

FRAME 7

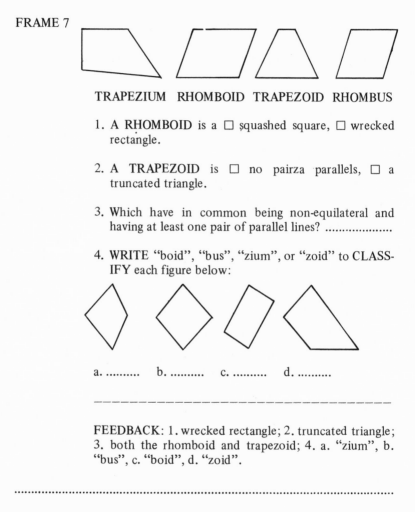

TRAPEZIUM   RHOMBOID   TRAPEZOID   RHOMBUS

1. A RHOMBOID is a ☐ squashed square, ☐ wrecked rectangle.

2. A TRAPEZOID is ☐ no pairza parallels, ☐ a truncated triangle.

3. Which have in common being non-equilateral and having at least one pair of parallel lines? ....

4. WRITE "boid", "bus", "zium", or "zoid" to CLASSIFY each figure below:

a. ....   b. ....   c. ....   d. ....

_____

FEEDBACK: 1. wrecked rectangle; 2. truncated triangle; 3. both the rhomboid and trapezoid; 4. a. "zium", b. "bus", c. "boid", d. "zoid".

....

FRAME 8   RHOMBOIDS—non-equilateral, non-right-angled, parallelograms

RHOMBUSES—equilateral, non-right-angled, parallelograms

TRAPEZOIDS—non-equilateral, non-right-angled, 1 pair parallels

TRAPEZIUMS–non-equilateral, non-right-angled, 0 pairs parallels

CLASSIFY each figure below by writing the correct term:

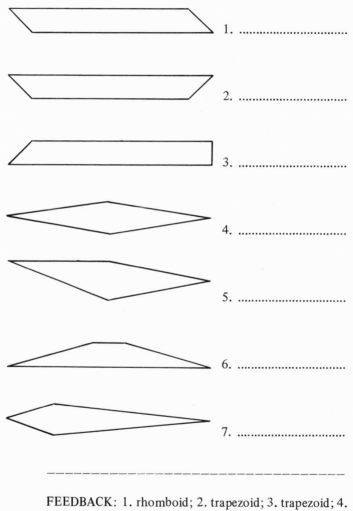

1. ....

2. ....

3. ....

4. ....

5. ....

6. ....

7. ....

FEEDBACK: 1. rhomboid; 2. trapezoid; 3. trapezoid; 4. rhombus; 5. trapezium; 6. trapezoid; 7. trapezium.

FRAME 9

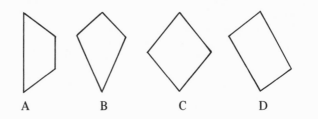

A   B   C   D

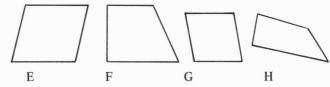

E   F   G   H

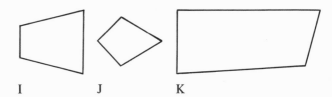

I   J   K

CIRCLE letters below to classify each figure:

1. RHOMBOIDS   A B C D E F G H I J K

2. RHOMBUSES   A B C D E F G H I J K

3. TRAPEZOIDS   A B C D E F G H I J K

4. TRAPEZIUMS   A B C D E F G H I J K

FEEDBACK: 1. D, G; 2. C, E; 3. A, F, I; 4. B, H, J, K.

FRAME 10 [A NUMBER OF RECTILINEAR QUADRILATE-RALS–SQUARES, RECTANGLES, RHOMBOIDS, RHOMBUSES, TRAPEZOIDS, AND TRAPEZIUMS–EACH WITH AN IDENTIFYING LETTER.]

Above are examples of quadrilaterals, each of which can be classified into one or more of the following categories: parallelogram, rectangle, rhomboid, rhombus, square, trapezium, trapezoid.

CLASSIFY each figure by writing next to its identifying letter below EACH CATEGORY into which it fits:

A. ....

ETC.

DONALD H. BULLOCK, Ph.D. (Psychology, Columbia University, 1950) is presently Senior Consultant, Performance Design Corporation, an affiliate of Harless Performance Guild, Inc., where his primary responsibilities are training needs analysis and the development of performance-based instruction and job aids. He first became involved with programmed instruction in 1961 as Manager, Programmed Teaching, Auerbach Corporation. His subsequent experience includes a variety of performance and instructional technology applications working with such organizations as Basic Systems Incorporated, Xerox Education Division, New Century Publications, Media Medica, Trenton, N.J. Board of Education, Metropolitan Educational Council for Staff Development, Communications Workers of America, U.S. Postal Service Training and Development Institute, Center for Educational Development in Health—Harvard School of Public Health, and others.

He spent a year in Sweden as Associate Professor of Educational Psychology, Institute of Education, Gothenburg University; and was for four years Professor of Education and Director, Center for Educational Technology, School of Education, The Catholic University of America, Washington, D.C.

Among his contributions to programmed instruction have been his direction of the programming of a number of self-instructional programs: *COBOL, Allergy and Hypersensitivity, Current Concepts of Thyroid Disease, You and Your Diabetes, Job Oriented Skills for High School Students,* and *Editing/Revising Programs for Self-Instruction* (co-authored with Vivian Wilson) are illustrative.

He served as Editor of the *NSPI Journal,* 1971-72; and was President Elect, President, and Past President, 1973-75 of the National Society for Performance and Instruction (NSPI).